A NEW VITALITY IN GENERAL EDUCATION

PLANNING, TEACHING, AND SUPPORTING
EFFECTIVE LIBERAL LEARNING
BY THE TASK GROUP ON GENERAL EDUCATION

JOSEPH KATZ
Chair
Professor of Human Development
State University of New York–
Stony Brook

LAURA BORNHOLDT
Special Assistant to the President
University of Chicago

JERRY G. GAFF
Acting Presiden
Hamline Univ

NANCY HOFFⁿ
Professor of Humaⁱ
University of Massachuset

LUCILE F. NEWMA
Associate Professor of Community Health
and Anthropology
Brown University

MARK RATNER
Professor of Chemistry
Northwestern University

RUDOLPH H. WEINGARTNER
Provost
University of Pittsburgh

ASSOCIATION OF AMERICAN COLLEGES, 1988

THE WORK OF THE TASK GROUP
ON GENERAL EDUCATION
WAS SUPPORTED
BY THE EXXON EDUCATION FOUNDATION
AND THE JOHNSON FOUNDATION.

Cover: *Memory Swirls*
Computer-generated art
by Barbara Nessim, ©1986.
As reproduced in
Digital Visions: Computers and Art
by Cynthia Goodman
©1987 Harry N. Abrams and Everson Museum.

Published by
Association of American Colleges
1818 R Street, NW
Washington, D.C. 20009

ISBN 0-911696-41-5

CONTENTS

INTRODUCTION

Much has been written about general education, but this publication differs from most others on the topic. We believe that the terms of discussion about general education need to be redefined and enlarged if the academic community is to move beyond cyclically recurring calls for reform to changes of real consequence. We focus on both the rationale, purposes, and scope of general education and on issues of implementation—specifically on effective ways of planning programs and courses, teaching them, and supporting them.

We have much to build on. Dean Curtis Ellison of Miami University in Ohio gave one reason for this document when he told us, "Examples of good educational practice are not as scarce as is good information about them." This publication provides information on a variety of examples of good educational practice with the hope that faculty and administrators can use it in creating more effective programs and reducing the chances of failure. It makes many suggestions about further improvements, but does not advocate a prescriptive uniformity. It seeks to stimulate reflection about general education in ways that respect the individuality and diversity of America's institutions of higher learning.

We see this document as building on the 1985 report of the Association of American Colleges, *Integrity in the College Curriculum*, and as one step in a collaborative effort in which faculty, administrators, and students can all participate in bringing about general education through the medium of the college—an institution imperfectly shaped to fulfill this purpose and yet the best available instrument for accomplishing it.

While the Task Group on General Education is alone responsible for this report, its work has benefited from the thoughtful recommendations of an advisory board consisting of:

William B. Boyd, President, Johnson Foundation
John W. Chandler, President, Association of American Colleges
Mark H. Curtis, President Emeritus, Association of American Colleges
Arthur Levine, President, Bradford College
Kenneth P. Mortimer, Vice President and Vice Provost, Pennsylvania State University

It also has benefited from the editorial advice of J. B. Hefferlin of the California Postsecondary Education Commission and Carol Schneider, Vice President of the Association of American Colleges. James Redfield of the University of Chicago actively participated in the early deliberations of the task group. The following individuals met at the Wingspread Conference Center of the Johnson Foundation on March 19–21, 1987, to consider an early draft of this publication from the perspective of their efforts in general education in their institutions and made many valuable suggestions:

Antioch University
President Alan Guskin

Bennington College
President Elizabeth Coleman

Brooklyn College
Professor Nancy Hager
President Robert L. Hess
Professor Charlton M. Lewis

Chicago State University
President George E. Ayers
Assistant Professor Jacquelyn S. Blackmon
Professor Magne B. Olsen
Professor Wesley Teo

Colorado College
Dean David D. Finlay
Professor John Riker
Professor James Yaffe

Gustavus Adolphus College
Professor Thomas A. Gover
President John S. Kendall
Professor Barbara Simpson

Miami University
Provost E. Fred Carlisle
Dean Curtis W. Ellison
Professor Philip A. Macklin

Tougaloo College
Professor Gerald V. Bruno
Associate Dean Bernice Coar-Cobb
Associate Professor Stephen L. Rozman

University of Minnesota
Professor Bonnie Pechtel
Professor Earl Shaw
Assistant Vice President John Wallace

University of Tennessee – Knoxville
Professor Gary N. Dicer
Professor W. Lee Humphreys
Associate Professor Marian Moffett

University of Wisconsin – River Falls
Dr. Charles Neff

Wheaton College (Massachusetts)
Professor Darlene L. Boroviak
Provost Hannah Goldberg

The Johnson Foundation
William B. Boyd, President
Henry Halsted, Vice President
Kay Mauer, Conference Coordinator

Wingspread Fellows
Alice E. Biggers (Aurora University)
Michelle Noel (North Central College)

We are indebted to the Exxon Education Foundation and to the Johnson Foundation for their generous support of the work of the Task Group.

[signature: Joseph Katz]

Joseph Katz
Chair, Task Group on
General Education

[signature: John W. Chandler]

John W. Chandler
President, Association of
American Colleges

PLANNING EFFECTIVE GENERAL EDUCATION

RETHINKING THE CONTENT
IDENTIFYING ESSENTIAL SKILLS
NEW CONTENT AND COMPETENCIES
CREATING NEW COURSES AND PROGRAMS
INTEGRATING CONTENT AND INQUIRY

We define general education as the cultivation of the knowledge, skills, and attitudes that all of us use and live by during most of our lives—whether as parents, citizens, lovers, travelers, participants in the arts, leaders, volunteers, or good samaritans.

Ideally one's knowledge, skills, and attitudes should continue developing throughout life. Yet knowledge and skills can stagnate and attitudes be reduced to stereotype, cliché, and prejudice. Thus the general education offered by colleges and universities seeks to foster the desire and capacity to keep on learning continuously. Through their general education programs, academic institutions aim to develop habits of and tastes for independent thinking by encouraging active learning and independent investigation, and by helping students assume responsibility for their own intellectual development. These programs exist above all to prevent stagnation of perception and to vivify thought and action through continuing reflection.

The chief task of the college years is for students ... to learn how to think about thinking and to enjoy thinking

Even without attending college, some young adults can lay the foundations for lives continually rich in thought and expressiveness. Literature abounds with illustrations, particularly in the *bildungsroman*, of how young women and men have developed their reflective powers and stature through their own deliberate observation of people, places, and ideas. Their self-education points to ways that educational institutions can aid this process among their students by developing their desire for wide-ranging reading, reflection, and exploration of intellectual connections throughout life. Intellectual power can be acquired if persistently practiced in and out of the classroom, yet it must become a matter of taste. As Aristotle would have it, pleasure must accompany its exercise.

Thus we believe that the chief task of the college years is for students not only to gain the ability to identify perspectives, weigh evidence, and make wise decisions, but also to learn how to think about thinking and to enjoy thinking. Students who have done so have crossed the great divide between merely gaining knowledge in order to return it on examinations and using knowledge by making it their own. Effective general education challenges students to confront both the complexity of knowing and the tentativeness of our knowledge.

This approach to general education requires a different style from that used in most departments for teaching their specialties. The study of specialized subject matter often aims at an increasingly refined investigation of progressively smaller areas of reality. General education is epistemologically different in that it aims at the cultivation of a complex intelligence—the capacity that George Santayana had in mind when he wrote the *Life of Reason*, exploring intelligence in art, religion, science, society, and common sense. Indeed, the vitality of nonspecialist perception probably is an important ingredient in keeping specialist thinking alive. The acquisition of a finely tuned method is no insurance against routine and tepid thought.

Well-conceived general education fosters the ability to formulate questions that point toward new knowledge and new directions for action. It seeks to provide, in the words of a committee at St. Joseph's University in Philadelphia, "the means for students to exercise control over their lives through thoughtful response to their political, cultural, and natural environments."[1] To work toward this objective calls for sustained imagination and daring on the part of faculty, students, and administrators, since many existing institutional policies and practices are incompatible with them. It requires faculty who are willing to practice fresh approaches to their teaching, students who are unafraid of challenging and even risk-taking experiences, and administrators who measure their institutions' effectiveness by the intellectual habits and intellectual range students acquire as undergraduates and the intellectual pursuits they pursue after they graduate. Most urgently, it requires rethinking educational content and attention to individual competence and skills.

RETHINKING THE CONTENT

General education involves many tensions: between what to teach and how to teach it, between the great classics of the past and contemporary works, between the classroom and students' out-of-class life, between students' individual objectives and the needs of the community, between what students want and what their institutions think they need, and between its means and ends—that is, between its reality of daily assignments and its goal of fostering the desire and capacity to continue learning. Among these tensions are issues of content. Few faculty are satisfied, even in our more prestigious institutions, with the level of student preparation. In most institutions, discussions of general education center on areas of content and, most often, on the best selection and arrangement of that common knowledge said to define the educated person. As faculty, we

repeatedly debate what specific "great" or "important" writings must be studied by students in order for them to be declared generally educated.

But what knowledge should we emphasize, and what should we require of all students? Most everyone would agree with the assertion of the National Endowment for the Humanities that "some things are more important to know than others," even though reaching agreement about which things are more important can be frustratingly difficult. In former centuries, the Bible provided for a shared frame of reference that could help communication among students and faculty of many different origins and dispositions. Now, however, the task of building a shared culture and some commonality of intellectual experience within an institution has no similar underpinning. We know from our work with undergraduates that a popular television program such as "General Hospital" or "Hill Street Blues" binds together students across the nation. Cannot then some common intellectual experiences bind together at least the students within an institution?

Some champions of a common core argue that all college students should have a solid grounding in the Western humanist tradition best embodied in a list of books beginning with Homer, Sophocles, Thucydides, and Plato and going forward to

Nietzsche, Mann, and T. S. Eliot. At some institutions, the great thinkers of Western civilization have been the *pièce de résistance* of higher education. To others, such a list seems at best limited and at worst an attempt to deny power to ideas emanating from classes that are not upper, races that are not white, cultures that are not Western, and everyone who is not male.

Faculty members in many institutions have sidestepped such seemingly insoluble disputes by establishing general education as a series of distribution requirements, a minimal sampling of disciplines offered more or less willingly by departments. Others have relied on interdisciplinary work to balance disciplinary specialization. And at still others, the "common-body-of-knowledge" approach has been challenged by faculty who emphasize the abilities, skills, competencies, modes of thought, and methods of access to knowledge that students should acquire to pursue investigation independently. Such programs may ask students to write coherent English, to think logically and analytically, to handle information couched in quantitative terms, to acquire historical consciousness, to master a language other than English with proficiency, and to examine or even to acquire values.

In later sections of this publication, we make a case for programs and teaching that focus on specific competencies and abilities that students are expected to develop during their four years in college. But competence in modes of inquiry and in writing does not develop in a vacuum. Thinking is always *about* something, and therefore it is inextricably grounded in content. Thus the question of which content to emphasize must be joined because the choice is inevitable and decisions must be made.

We need, therefore, to deliberate carefully about what college-educated Americans should know and be able to do in the remaining years of the twentieth century and the early decades of the twenty-first. The question is particularly complex because the student body is no longer a homogeneous elite; instead, it varies along virtually all the dimensions on which it is possible for people to differ: age, race, sex, social and economic background, abilities, attitudes, ambitions, and goals.

Despite the diversity in our student bodies—indeed, because of it—we believe that all students can benefit from a common intellectual experience. At a minimum, colleges and universities can select one major text and ask that it be read and intensively discussed both by all students and by all faculty members in an institution. Such a requirement communicates to students and to faculty that they are all members of a community committed both to inquiry and to communication about the results of inquiry. It requires faculty members to consider what issues extend beyond particular fields and are significant for the larger community.

We also believe that colleges and universities can make a commitment to a more ambitious program of common learning. An enduring and adaptable common learning experience is possible when the members of a community make a serious commitment to sustain it. For instance, Columbia University's Contemporary Civilization course has been a part of its curriculum since the First World War.

Programs of common learning should cut across disciplinary or departmental boundaries. General education has too often been defined—or negotiated—in terms of existing departments rather than by an examination of what constitutes good education. Faculty discussions of content have frequently been political in nature, controlled by considerations of departmental turf. Such political debates displace the discussions we ought to be having—discussions about the intellectual needs of our students and about the kinds of competence most important for them. When we start with departmental turf as our frame of reference, we miss the opportunity to help our students explore potential linkages and complementaries across disciplines and subjects.

One way to approach the development of a general education program is to consider the meaning and value of our common life and our responsibility to and for each other as human beings. Living in a technological revolution, in times of great social transformation, under the threat of nuclear war and diseases with no known cure, and visited daily by graphic images of desperate poverty within plenty, we can decide that issues such as these are as important for our students to understand and act on as are the technical skills for a career. To participate knowledgeably in civic affairs, young adults need mastery of data, theory, commentary, and argument in these problem areas. Well-informed citizens and family members require knowledge about such complex issues as toxic waste disposal, redistribution of income, medical care, and the emotional health of individuals and groups. College students do not learn about these major dilemmas just because they are important. Many students do not even read a daily newspaper or a weekly news magazine. Their information about contemporary issues may be limited to newsbreaks on their music stations.

The great books can find a ready place in a program devoted to such contemporary themes. After all, Plato's *Republic* was a grand attempt to reconstruct Athenian society after the Peloponnesian War, and many of Aristotle's writings were inspired by the desire to make democracy work in the political, legal, and social arenas. We need not set up an opposition between great classics and contemporary relevance. Good education requires continuing inquiry into the relationship between the two. For example, the core curriculum at CUNY–Brooklyn College, filling just over one-quarter of its students' program, deliberately encompasses both the old and the new, the traditional and the contemporary. Students taking it are expected to encounter both the enduring legacies of Western culture and the contemporary perspectives offered by modern science, computer technology, and attention to non-Western studies. If we believe that the great books continue to speak to participants in our own society, then we must help students see the connections between the questions raised in these books and the problems they will confront as persons and as citizens. Too often we neglect such connections, sometimes in the belief that the students will make these links for themselves, sometimes in the belief that it demeans a great work to discuss it out of its originating context. Yet the result of this neglect is that many students see classic works as an imposition to be endured rather than a resource for their own lives. General education programs can and

should leave students with effective models for how to draw on the rich resources of our culture in pursuing further learning.

To serve this purpose, we believe attempts to constitute a general education program as a conglomerate of disciplinary courses fall short of the mark. Both students and faculty members benefit when they are challenged to think about the connections among ideas and issues across disciplinary and departmental boundaries.

Similarly, we believe it is unwise to define general education in terms of the traditional division between general learning and specialized learning in a field of concentration. This long-standing distinction between general learning and the major creates a misleading and artificial boundary. For many undergraduates, and especially for those who major in liberal arts disciplines, the fields in which they do their undergraduate work are not directly related to their eventual occupations. Thus their major is often part of their general education rather than preparation for a professional career. Like many graduates of former decades who eventually found themselves in fields that did not exist when they were in college, many of today's students will have careers in occupations that presently do not exist. And unlike students in most other countries, many American students do not enter postsecondary education with a specialty firmly in mind. For many of them, the entire college experience is general education.

For those students who go on to work professionally in the field of their undergraduate concentration, it is equally important that there be broad, integrative dimensions to their study in the major. Whatever their chosen field, study in the major should help students place their particular academic commitments in larger intellectual, historical, and cultural perspectives.

Specialized study of any major can and should be infused with broader meanings and purposes. Too often, however, the traditional dichotomy between liberal or general versus departmental or technical education polarizes virtually all deliberations about the college curriculum. As Elizabeth Coleman has written:

If a course is entitled "Nietzsche, Marx, and Freud," it is for freshmen. If it is "Marx and Freud," it is for sophomores. If it is "Freud," it is for juniors and seniors. And if it is "Freud: The Case Studies," it is a graduate course. I would hope that the assumptions this locks us into regarding the education of freshmen as well as seniors could be examined. I would hope that we could even see that "Freud: The Case Studies" might be a powerful introductory course; just as I hope it is manifestly absurd to de-emphasize the activities of integration and synthesis for seniors.[2]

In this spirit, we regard the introductory course in a discipline as an important aspect of general education. The introductory course, whether in a liberal arts subject or in a professional field, ought to become an object of special attention in planning general education. To whom does it introduce what? Many students who select an introductory level course will never take another course in the discipline, so it clearly does not introduce them to further formal work in the field. One special goal of such a course should therefore be some guidance to these students about how they can continue learning in the discipline on their own.

The need to teach one's discipline to students not majoring in it provides a special opportunity for investigating the ways in which that discipline illuminates the problems and questions of our common life. Exploring the role of the course in these students' overall intellectual life need not lead to diluting content. Instead, it can show how the course provides a framework for dealing with intellectually challenging questions that non-specialists raise or may be induced to raise about the discipline.

In planning introductory courses we might well consider how immersion in particular discipline shapes one's mind. As faculty members, we have so long been imbued with the thoughtways of our disciplines that

Exploration of the competencies that we as faculty wish our students to achieve is an indispensable prerequisite for planning general education curricula

we may have lost touch with how we learned to think like scientists or scholars, while first-year students tend to be unaware that academic languages are rather like foreign tongues. Currently, methods courses that are explicit about disciplinary thinking—the "how" of the disciplines—are ordinarily reserved for upper-level majors who are being trained to do research. But aspects of these methods courses should be introduced into the design of many introductory and other courses to teach students to think about thinking and about the differences in the ways in which historians, scientists, or literary critics think about the same issues.

It is a challenging but essential task for faculty members to reflect on what shape they want their introductory course to take, fully acknowledging the fact that for many students this one course will be the only exposure to their discipline. Such reflection is likely to raise basic questions about the nature of the discipline itself, its focus, and its explanatory power. Moreover, by exploring how their course fits in with courses in other subjects, faculty members are likely to find themselves in searching discussions with their colleagues about the connectedness and disconnectedness of subject matters and methods of inquiry. The outcome of such deliberations is not likely to be a unified corpus of scholarship and

science. But the discussions themselves are likely to take faculty and students out of disciplinary isolation and toward a spirited inquiry into the foundations, boundaries, and linkages of their disciplines. It may even lead to some reconceptualization of their own disciplines.

IDENTIFYING ESSENTIAL SKILLS

We propose that when faculty committees rethink general education programs and when instructors plan their own individual courses, they define not only subject matter and readings but also the skills they wish students to practice and develop—specifically, what their students should be able to perceive and do as a result of the program and of the particular courses within it. Skills and competencies cannot be nurtured outside the study of particular contents, but we too often plan contents with insufficient reference to skills beyond those of memorization and recall. A recent study of liberal arts college faculty showed that while they overwhelmingly aimed at encouraging independent thinking, nearly half of their examination questions involved the regurgitation of course content.[3]

Exploration of the competencies that we as faculty wish our students to achieve is an indispensable prerequisite for planning general education curricula. Defining these competencies helps achieve integration of under-graduate courses and enables students to graduate with an identifiable sense of achievement. By identifying and describing the specific competencies our courses require, we are taking the first steps toward making our ways of thinking, including the thought patterns of our disciplines, explicit to each other and to students. When spelled out in sufficient detail, skills statements expose the inner workings of academic disciplines. As an illustration, consider the skills defined in the Harvard core curriculum statement on literature and arts:

The common aim of courses in this area [Literature and Arts] is to help students develop a critical understanding of how human beings give artistic expression to their experience of the world. Through the examination of selected works, students are expected to enlarge and refine skills of reading, seeing, and hearing; to understand the possibilities and limitations of the artists' chosen medium and the means available for expression; and to appreciate the complex interplay among individual talent, artistic tradition, and historical context.[4]

The value of a statement like this is that it identifies the minimum literary critical skills to be acquired by Harvard students, starting with improving their basic critical capacities, then moving to a consideration of artists' use of their materials, and

finally raising complex contextual issues of the individual, tradition, and history. It is the beginning of a statement about what literary critics and scholars do. It is a very different statement from one scientists or philosophers would make, just as it is a different statement from that of faculty who might add a more personal, experiential dimension to aesthetic understanding.

At the same time, the description just cited uses a vague set of terms—*understand, appreciate, enlarge, refine.* Moreover, terms such as *understand* and *appreciate* imply a student who looks in on the world of literature and the arts, rather than a student who actively engages problems, questions, and issues within these domains. Rather than relying on such terms, we can categorize skills so that they cover a hierarchy of abilities, from *describe* and *summarize* to *analyze, compare, critique, theorize,* and *extend theory.* Once we as faculty agree together on a definition of skills we look for as an outcome of learning in our fields, the clarity of our assignments and exams will improve. Our ability to pinpoint students' intellectual problems will also improve. Too often, when we have been charged to develop courses that will foster students' intellectual abilities, we have simply repackaged old courses—claiming, for example, that "World Music" leads to an understanding of "the possibilities and limitations of the artist's chosen medium."

Faculty at a handful of colleges, however, have become explicit not only about the meaning of each skill statement, but about how each skill or competence can be taught and how it can be documented. They have defined not only broad outcomes of general education, but "how much" and "how well." Most of these colleges tend to serve "new students"—first-generation college students, minority students, low-income students—students for whom the initiation into academic culture is most difficult. But these institutions have something to teach all of us. "New students" clearly benefit from the articulation of criteria and standards for judgment, but all students learn more effectively when agreement about skills replaces "psyching out" the professor.

A look at foreign language instruction illustrates the problems that arise when we give only secondary attention to the achievement of competency, even in a field for whose existence such achievement seems a primary objective. Most everyone would agree that languages are learned best by those who have a use for them. It is also commonly agreed that languages are best retained by those who bring them to some usable level, either for conversation or reading, and that this level can usually be reached only in a minimum of two years and for only a few languages. Yet many institutions do not require students to use a foreign language or even learn it, but merely study it. Often, colleges require only one year's study of a language. If our goal is to have a large number of students take one year of a language in college and no more, we should design courses accordingly. For instance, it is possible to teach students to read Homer sensitively in a year of ordinary course work without their achieving general proficiency in Greek. But whatever we do, we should define what is to be learned and how—and decide what are realistic objectives and what are not.

Faculty members who want to think about the competencies important to their courses may find studies of intellectual development a useful point of departure. The investigations of Jean Piaget and William Perry in particular have been helpful to many faculty groups interested in understanding intellectual development and its intersection with the development of competence in particular fields or courses.[5] Piaget's distinction between "concrete" and "formal" operations leads us to investigate what sort of practices are necessary to enable students to tell the difference between "fact" and "interpretation." In the words of one student, "a fact is what the teacher says it is." This is true for a learner who has not yet learned to work with abstractions, that is, to operate at a "formal" level with the issues of a field. Such students will find it difficult to grapple with discussions or assignments that presuppose the ability to infer organizing principles from particular data to deal with the relations among the principles.

William Perry's research on the intellectual and ethical development of Harvard students across the four years of college has given us a thoughtful scheme of nine "positions" through which the thinking of college students advances. Perry's scheme begins with an authority-bound phase in which students look for the right answer and want to be told, rather than investigate. When they find out that answers to many problems are tentative and controversial, they move into a position Perry terms "multiplicity," in which one opinion seems as good as the other, their own and the teacher's included. Students can be challenged to move beyond this subjectivism through the discovery that there are competent and incompetent ways to gather evidence and develop and test hypotheses. Then they can learn that while there are no final certitudes, there are ways to develop responsible, disciplined, and flexible theories and positions. At the heart of Perry's work and that of other observers of student intellectual development is a powerful

yet simple observation: Students gain intellectual sophistication when they must confront and assess competing and equally well-argued perspectives on an issue or solutions to a problem.

Attention to intellectual skills and competencies puts emphasis on the outcomes of education. Most college transcripts certify that students have passed a required number of courses, but they give little indication of the competencies that students have developed. A focus on competencies is likely to engender lively debate among faculty about the nature of these competencies, which of them are essential, and how they may best be developed. It is also likely to increase student interest in general education. Currently, one of the great virtues of professional education as contrasted to general education is that students carry from it a sense of at least incipient empowerment through their attainment of specific skills. Too many students graduate from college with an uncomfortable sense that the knowledge they have acquired outside their specialty is vague and diffuse. General education that is more deliberately and explicitly geared to the development of competencies defined independently of the passing of individual courses can change their perceptions greatly.

The very prolificness of the research emanating from women's studies attests to the power of the questions it is raising and the methods it is employing

NEW CONTENT AND COMPETENCIES

In this section we single out two examples of new approaches to content and competencies: women's studies and general education science courses. Women's studies has a twenty-year history of challenging what were once viewed as accepted ideas and practices, and it is transforming our basic ways of understanding social, psychological, and historical processes. In contrast, general education science courses have long been a traditional part of the higher education curriculum. However, both women's studies and general education science courses illustrate opportunities for engaging students in work that imparts new content, provides new skills, and clarifies values.

Women's studies introduced areas of content—classes of people and their past and present activities—that had been excluded from scholarly inquiry in fields ranging from biology to the history of art. It made the everyday, domestic, emotional, and interpersonal sides of people's lives the subject of intensive exploration and analysis and thus considerably enlarged the comprehensiveness and objectivity of our knowledge. It has pursued the questions raised by the influx of women into the labor force around the world—one of the most profound social changes in recent history—such issues as comparable worth, affirmative action, and distribution of child care responsibilities.

These new questions have provided a powerful stimulus for fresh approaches in the classroom. They are questions of great complexity where student and faculty emotions are strong, where there is no "correct" or traditional approach to problem solving, where unknown content must be uncovered, and where new ways of thinking are required. Faculty have used the intensity of student involvement in the issues as opportunities for having students realize the importance and the power of thinking clearly. The questioning of accepted explanations of topics and problems which has been at the core of the development of women's studies as a field has motivated an emphasis on accurate description, analysis, synthesis, and theory building. The very prolificness of the research emanating from women's studies attests to the power of the questions it is raising and the methods it is employing. Students are exposed to the intellectual excitement of creating a new field of study.

Women's studies programs have often functioned as thorns in the side of traditional departments, pointing out facts—inequities in numbers, salary, and tenure patterns for women faculty—and moving institutions, and the society beyond, to reveal the degree to which they were wedded to maintaining the inequities with which they were confronted. Women's studies has in fresh ways raised the ancient question of the relationship of knowledge to personal and social action.

At this time, there are about five hundred academic programs, some thirty-nine thousand women's studies courses—usually taken as electives or as part of general education—and several refereed journals devoted to scholarship on women. These activities include extensive projects designed to integrate women's studies across the curriculum, a special literature on the philosophy and tactics of curricular change, and an explosion of scholarly work in many disciplines.

The growing literature about women's studies shows that women's studies can be seen as a way of rethinking general education. In a review essay, Margaret Andersen cites five phases of curricular evolution.[6] First, there is the "womanless" curriculum, the curriculum that presents the world as if women were invisible. Second, a few and highly successful women begin to appear; their achievements are added. Third, with the development of extensive scholarship on women's lives and work, women take their place as a group beside men. In phase four, changes in ways of knowing begin to appear. The curriculum reveals a new organization and perspective. It in-

vestigates cultural functions, such as affiliation, or understudied aspects of men's lives, such as their emotional lives and nurturant activities. Thinking necessarily becomes more interdisciplinary. Finally, as full transformation is approached, difference and diversity of human experience, sex, race, class, and ethnicity are seen as part of the continuum of human experience, and this introduces a profound shift in world view. While some institutions are still at phase one, others, like Wheaton College in Massachusetts, have undertaken institution-wide curriculum revision.

We turn to the natural sciences as our second example. The task group gave special attention to this domain because the natural sciences comprise an area that is commonly regarded as particularly resistant to general education. Discussions of curricular practices in the sciences and of ways to improve them have often been unsatisfying and evanescent. Yet the technological society in which we live is faced with challenges and choices ranging from the preservation of plant and animal life to the control of nuclear power, toxic wastes, and devastatingly powerful weaponry. While our current standard of living is largely based on science and technology, the American public, including much of its political leadership, is both ill-educated in science and intimidated by technology.

How can the general lack of scientific understanding in American society be explained? Some insight into our failure can be gleaned from an examination of the paradigms for college science courses and the difficulties that beset them:

☐ The broad but isolated survey, perhaps entitled "Scientific Ideas of Western Society," that omits experimental experience and emphasizes instead anecdotal history rather than methodological or epistemological issues, and whose scientific content may be minimal.

☐ The watered-down course, possibly named "Physics for Poets" or "Life Sciences for Nonmajors," that lacks the courage to make the students work on real scientific questions.

☐ The historical methodology course, possibly called "Methods of Modern Physics" or "Microscopies, Old and New," that seems very "scientific" in its emphasis on the specific, but is devoted to instruments rather than to modes of thought.

☐ The intensive professional course, such as "Introduction to Physics" or "General Chemistry." These courses may be the appropriate vehicle for getting a great store of technique and knowledge across to future engineers, scientists, and pre-medical students, but they lack continuity with the thinking and the everyday experience of most other students. Indeed, these courses help to convince many students that their negative preconceptions about science were right when the great ideas they have been promised turn out to be a set of formulas designed to tell how fast an elevator falls or which acids ionize weakly.

A properly constructed general education in science allows students to understand the generality, power, and coherence of nature's fundamental principles. To do so, the courses stress methodology, thought patterns, and the nature of those principles themselves. They also stress two other central elements: factual and descriptive knowledge, and an ability to know and use quantitative concepts. The facts remain critical, since conceptualization in the absence of concrete detail risks sterility and vacuousness, just as detail in the absence of concept risks chaos. Such a course in physics can measure acceleration, sound propagation, and magnetic fields. One in chemistry can demonstrate reactions and heat, smells, and solutions. One in geology can dwell on the dynamics and the details of rock formation in the earth's crust.

Science education can equip students to understand reasonable orders of magnitude for physical quantities and to appreciate the process of numerical size estimation and the nature of statistical and probabilistic descriptions. Many of the issues facing our society are clarified immediately if subjected to scrutiny on the basis of reliable estimation. The educated person should be able to criticize the more relevant numerical estimates to which the media constantly subject us, whether they are opinion polls, the chance of winning a lottery, the probability of a catastrophic earthquake, the danger of a meltdown, or risks of cancer from exposure to certain chemicals. Many instances of well-intentioned legislation, regulation, and crying of woe are based on inaccurate estimates. Numbers must be used with knowledge and respect, and measurement must be viewed in the context of theory and of answers to intrinsically important intellectual and socially relevant questions.

In practice, most coursework in science is didactic. Facts and theories are presented, often very well, and ways to derive predictions from these facts and theories are taught. But students need help in reestablishing the contexts out of which scientific questions arise along with the "answers" which at any time constitute the contents of science. One way to provide this help involves the use of paradoxes. Demonstrations that begin with paradoxes challenge students to go beyond their original instincts to gain a deeper and more sophisticated knowledge, and can inspire them to pursue explanatory clues by which they learn the underlying science.
□ Why doesn't the water spill out of a glass that is filled above its brim with water? What happens if lighter fluid or mineral oil or alcohol is used instead?
□ Why does a sheet of paper spread across the top of a glass of milk keep the milk in when the glass is overturned? Will it still work in a vacuum?
□ Why doesn't a tennis ball floating under the spigot in a bathtub float away?
□ Why does the size seven shoe lying to the right of the size six look smaller?
These paradoxes help students learn first that initial feeling and empirical guesswork can be very dangerous if incautiously employed, second that measurement or experiment is a proper way to answer a well-posed question, and third that scientific learning and knowledge are not only useful but delightful.

The use of projects can also play an invigorating role in science courses addressed to the general education of students. Through properly chosen and even self-selected projects, students will become more divergent and more independent in their thought, and more aware both of how method can determine action and of how concept development imbues specific facts with meaning and comprehensibility. Classroom presentations can then be organized in concert with these project components so that students perceive the formal presentation of course materials as providing an organized set of constructs with which to order the observations that they themselves have made. For example, after students have observed pollen grains in water, and have noticed that the excursive motions are affected by the temperature of the water and by the size of the grain, the instructors have before them fertile, well-prepared mental ground in which to sow the seminal ideas of viscous drag, random motion, and molecular chaos.

To meet the larger goals of stimulating inquiry and imagination, and to offer opportunities for direct student involvement in scientific reasoning, science courses may be constructed around one or another major theme. For purposes of illustration, consider a possible course entitled "Rates of Change"—a course based on the measurement and understanding of rate phenomena and on linking the concept of equilibrium states to the rate processes by which the equilibrium eventuates. Such a course could begin with discussion of the nature of time and of measurements of rates such as the speed of a runner. The teacher would explain why these are important questions and how this type of inquiry is used in scientific research. The teacher could then carry through one simple demonstration, such as measuring the dependence of yeast fermentation rates on sugar concentration, and the students would design and complete their first measurement projects. In analyzing their observations, the students are introduced into the graphical presentation of data, the use of computers, and the treatment of a qualitative concept through quantitative data.

□ The next part of the course could be the most challenging, both for the instructor and students. Rather than baldly state such ideas as dynamic equilibrium, the principle of mass action, the differential and integral forms of rate laws, and the idea of limiting behaviors, the teacher can use the students' own lab findings to motivate them as well as illustrate these concepts. For instance, the statistical nature of equilibria and the Boltzmann picture of entropy can be illustrated by the movement of guppies in aquaria. The students can be assigned the analysis of each other's data in terms of rate laws and equilibrium constants.

□ In the last part of the course, the simple concepts of rate processes can be tested, both in discussion and in the laboratory, by comparison with more complex phenomena. These can include oscillatory rate processes, first as simple as a marble rolling in a mixing bowl but then proceeding to chemical oscillations, ecological oscillations, and circadian rhythms. Finally, the energetic consequences of rate phenomena can be measured, and catalytic reduction of barriers studied.

To our knowledge, no such course has ever been taught. But each of its parts is currently offered in other courses. By combining them, the course would fulfill almost all of the criteria for a general education course in science, including attention to methodology, thought pattern, factual and descriptive knowledge, and the use of quantitative concepts.

The life sciences offer another opportunity to involve in scientific reasoning students who believe that they dislike or fear science. These students can mobilize natural curiosities about their own bodies and the larger biosphere to form a base for coursework. A one- or two-semester course in biology could be created around any of a number of themes such as the biology of inherited disease. This course could cover classical principles of genetics; molecular aspects of genetics; diseases and malfunctions; and include a laboratory component involving exercises, model experiments, and investigative projects. Several of the most important conceptual bases of science can be examined in this course, among them the mechanism of evolution and of natural selection, or the concept of entropy by considerations of coding and of random as opposed to ordered codes. By evoking students' curiosity about disease with the power of discovery in the laboratory, such a course can provide opportunities for active learning. The instructor can further encourage active learning by making at least some of the formal presentations speculative and suggestive, emphasizing the range of questions still being pursued rather than that which seems presently established.

Such a course can accomplish these objectives:

□ The experimental work directly establishes the possible truth or clear falsehood of one or more hypotheses, and students are directly involved in the design and execution of the experiment.

□ The procedures are not technique exercises but laboratory studies measuring real properties of real species (eye color of flies, sickling of cells, sterility of offspring).

□ The facts are presented in the classroom, demonstrated in the preliminary lab work, and discovered in the investigative laboratory. Through observation, students learn important areas of content (osmotic excess can fracture cells, overdense populations can alter behavior), some of which can be directly useful in their lives.

□ Numerical estimation enters in a very natural way into some of the key concepts of the course. For instance, if one generation takes twenty-five years for humans but twenty-five hours for some organism, how many generations of each occur in ten thousand years? If a base pair has a mass of four hundred daltons, how many base pairs will fit on a DNA strand of mass three million daltons? By using rather than merely memorizing these concepts, the students acquire an appreciation for what numbers mean and how to manipulate them.

Orienting a general education course in science on such a theme has the virtue of providing a coherent framework without sacrificing knowledge of basic concepts and methods. Different teachers and institutions will naturally want to pick different themes. One physics professor reports that the heat death of the universe as a theme seems to appeal to most students at his college. At another institution, a biology professor is offering a basic biology course organized as the "Biology of Gender," which includes such areas as the evolution of plants and animals, social organization among primates and humans, and genetics. Offered to biology majors and nonmajors alike, she reports that the course helps to demystify science for the nonmajors and that the differing intellectual strengths and perspectives of the students make for richer, mutually instructive discussions.[7]

Science is an intellectual endeavor with many contextual ramifications from and into other modes of thought. Exploring these connections can play a central role in enriching, deepening, and focusing the education of all students. For science majors, general education is crucial since their specialties can be farther from ordinary experience than are the humanities or social sciences. Education that helps science majors place their special interests in larger contexts can make a fundamental difference in the ways these future scientists will think about the larger significance and implications of their work. Both science and scientists will fare best when closely interwoven into the general intellectual life of institutions and society.

CREATING NEW COURSES AND PROGRAMS

We believe that the process through which institutions answer the question of what content and competencies to emphasize can be a major educational experience for students and other constituencies. The question should be the subject of a visible, ongoing public discussion within institutions, involving faculty, students, administrators, and even alumni and governing boards, with the participation of community leaders, foundation officials, legislators, and other interested laypersons.

Such discussions can be enormously exciting intellectually, particularly if all faculty—whether biochemists, historians, computer scientists, or philosophers—engage the issues both as well-educated professionals and also as parents, spouses, friends, citizens, and neighbors. Equally important, students are seldom drawn into extended discussions of the underlying philosophies that lead us to establish their sequence of courses. They infrequently hear intellectual debate among faculty and even less frequently are given an opportunity to join in. Yet for many students, particularly those who have not previously thought of "ideas" as a source of power or playfulness, such an opportunity can make the difference between regarding education as a static thing to "get" and regarding it as a process of reflection and self-reflection leading to judgment, commitment, and action.

Discussions about general education can draw on the work of a variety of thinkers from varied fields, historical eras, and cultures, including recent reports on American higher education. These reports constitute a good inventory of current claims about the kinds of knowledge graduating college seniors should possess, and these claims can serve as the basis for extensive debate. In *Integrity in the College Curriculum*, the Association of American Colleges identified the following eight areas of experience that, together with "study in depth," are "basic to a coherent undergraduate education":

□ Inquiry, abstract logical thinking, critical analysis.
□ Literacy: writing, reading, speaking, listening.
□ Understanding numerical data.
□ Historical consciousness.
□ Science.
□ Values.
□ Art.
□ International and multicultural experiences.[8]

But if we look at the sum total of what has been proposed in the many reports, we come to realize that it is vastly greater than can be accomplished within the time that is available for a normal college education. At the same time, there is nothing in such lists that is undesirable, gratuitous, frivolous, or foolish. Every item has its partisans and its opponents. Arguments for adding to or subtracting from the list are deeply in conflict with each other, exhibiting disagreements both about the ends to be achieved and the means thought capable of bringing them about. We disagree about the pedagogic techniques that will bring about such desired results as rigorous thinking. We have difficulties bridging intellectually gaps that are rooted in profound cultural differences. Yet decisions must be made and we can make them at least on the basis of intelligent and thorough discussion. We will say more about ways to support such engagement in the third chapter. But we want to stress at the outset that the discus-

sion of these issues will be less en-
cumbered and the results more easily
implemented if institutions seek to
safeguard the economic status of professors who are willing to change the
contents and structures of their
courses.

To bring about new courses and
programs, faculty also need help in
renewing and expanding their skills.
Hamline University illustrates one
way of doing so: It has begun rethinking existing courses by initiating
a program of faculty renewal. Its
English department has pioneered the
process by organizing a seminar on
new methods of literary criticism that
have developed since its current
faculty members were in graduate
school. The entire department is
reading seminal works, discussing key
issues among themselves and with
consultants, and considering the contents of existing and new courses and
course sequences both for majors and
nonmajors.

Students also have an important
role not only in discussing general
education but in planning courses
and programs and assisting in moni-
toring them. To provide settings in
which students can take initiative to
formulate and test ideas, general education programs should include
opportunities for students to experience at least one course in which
they are in a special way in charge of
the content and methods of learning.

An example is furnished by Brown
University's Group Independent
Study Projects (GISPs), which allow
students to choose their own topics
for investigation. Subjects of student
projects have included environmental
pollutants, the effects of a family
member's cancer upon the family,
and the history and technology of
robotics. Students must submit de-
tailed outlines for their project, including a full bibliography, and each
project requires committee approval.
The students work together and
course contents and methods emerge
from their mutual collaboration.
Faculty members function as consultants, but the ways they are used
is determined by the students. At the
same time, the students' work is
judged by the faculty. The GISPs thus
facilitate the achievement of what is
essential in general education—the
development of the habits of and
tastes for independent investigation.

INTEGRATING CONTENT
AND INQUIRY

We believe that efforts to confine
general education to the first and second year of college are both chimeri-
cal and self-defeating. They assume
that freshmen, only starting their
exposure to the world of higher learning, can undertake syntheses that few
of their instructors could achieve;
and they make general education

appear to be an isolated activity—
requirements to be finished, gotten
out of the way, and then forgotten—
rather than a continuing progress of
growing throughout the years. In the
opening pages of this report, we
defined general education as the
cultivation of knowledge, skills, and
attitudes important to learning
throughout life. If we accept that
general education lays a foundation
for lifelong learning, then it needs to
be structured in such a way that it
fosters continuing learning.

The fostering of intellectual habits
and tastes as a central objective for
general education programs cannot
be accomplished in any single course
but requires collaborative efforts
across courses. A comprehensive plan
is necessary if individual competencies
are to form part of the student's
general intellectual and aesthetic
endowment. Yet a persistent com-
ment about faculty is that as a consequence of the domination of the
research model, we have specialized
to such a degree that we have lost
interest in and the capacity for integrating knowledge.

In most instances, students must do
their own synthesizing of knowledge.
Professors have offered their individual courses, perhaps with some link-
age to other courses in mind, and
then have relied on students to integrate the new knowledge into larger
structures of understanding. The

problem is that the logical coherence
among subjects is often neither shared
nor explicit. It exists in the mind of
Professor A, but Professor B constructs it differently, and the students
perceive a loose jumble. The students
often see little relation between one
course and another, and they frequently complain that the rationale
for their program eludes them. Integration calls for faculty to collaborate
with their colleagues and their students in linking courses toward
agreed-upon objectives.

Today, courses in different departments overlap in ways that may be
repetitive rather than building on
one another, and each of the overlap-
ping courses may be too narrowly
focused. Subspecialties of fields have
proliferated into hundreds of courses,
some so overblown that their substance does not require the amount
of time devoted to them, and others
so sketchy as to do an injustice to
the fields they presume to survey.
Equally bothersome is the neglect of
emerging new fields and the failure to
review critically existing courses
whose content and structure have
reached canonical status and that are
unjustifiably exempt from needing to
make a case for themselves.

We should look at courses in their
sequences and interrelations to see
that they build up to coherent competencies over the four years and to
allow students opportunities to prac-

Working on the connections
across fields or topics helps faculty
articulate the nature and the purpose
of nonspecialized knowledge
as well as teach it more effectively

tice and demonstrate these competencies. Inadequate attention to the place of individual courses in a student's total program is probably the single most important reason for the student's failure to achieve the competencies we hope for from their undergraduate education.

Leadership in this area has recently come from the writing community. As a consequence of their efforts, more and more institutions have begun to expect students to gain practice in writing in their courses across the disciplines and in a variety of genres in addition to academic research papers. Through these programs in "writing across the curriculum," both students and faculty members can gain insight into the varied ways that different fields frame, approach, and analyze questions. We would hope that ultimately this emphasis on writing as a competence to be practiced throughout the four years will lead not just to skill in articulation but to articulation with style.

Meanwhile, the principle reflected in the "writing across the curriculum" initiatives ought to be extended to many other important areas of student learning, such as critical thinking, problem solving, aesthetic experience, scientific literacy, and historical consciousness. Emphasizing such abilities throughout the undergraduate experience makes use of the psycho-

logical phenomenon of reinforcement. Reinforcement is crucial in education; people learn through repetition and encouragement as well as through inspiration and enlightenment.

Given the importance of reinforcement to learning, we can explore ways of using it to develop students' understanding of content as well as their competence in modes of inquiry. For example, faculty might plan to reintroduce certain topics or concepts with differing emphases or applications, at different times and in different contexts, over the four-year undergraduate cycle. We use the concept of entropy as an example.

□ The concept of entropy or disorder, the major quantitative aspect of the second law of thermodynamics, might be introduced as a historical and technological development based on Carnot and the steam engine, and then in the context of a general discussion of equilibrium.

□ This can be followed by laboratory experience in which the heat, entropy, and disorder changes that accompany the melting of an ice cube are measured.

□ Later, Boltzmann's formal definition of the disorder as exponential entropy might be discussed and used as the basis for determining the order of nature at the low temperatures of the interstellar medium.

□ Finally, the entropy changes characteristic of biological processes on the one hand and of economic and other social theory on the other could be calculated and discussed.

By seeing this difficult concept in various guises and at different stages in their careers, students are likely to become more confident both of their ability to comprehend an important central idea in science and of their capacity to deal mathematically with an abstract concept. For students who have completed most of their science and mathematical general education, an upper-level seminar on a concept such as entropy or evolution, combining faculty from several departments, can knit together work in various disciplines. It can also facilitate instructive contacts of students and faculty in different departments.

Many institutions are already linking courses and course content across the curriculum. For example, Colorado College has established a thematic minor: students take at least five courses—from two or more departments outside their major—which relate to one another through a common theme, area of the world, or historical period. Among two-year colleges that have pioneered the development of linked-course curricula, Los Medanos College in California requires students to take a minimum of one course in six major areas of knowledge, ranging from humanistic studies to physical sciences. To be included in the general education program, these courses

must give attention to reading and writing, modes of inquiry, aesthetics of knowledge, implications of knowledge, interdisciplinarity, effective thinking, and creativity. These courses are followed by two in-depth courses stressing critical inquiry and self-directed study. The Dallas County Community College district has defined eight competency areas that are not taught in a single course but are reinforced throughout the curriculum and in college degree requirements.

Another successful procedure for using the curriculum to link disciplines and stimulate debate among them has been developed in the Federated Learning Communities program at the State University of New York at Stony Brook. These communities group six courses that are already in the catalogue around a broad theme, such as world hunger, social and ethical issues in the life sciences, or the varied nature of communities. A group of students commit themselves to enroll in the six courses, three in each semester, and the faculty of the six courses meet regularly to discuss their courses and teaching efforts. These faculty jointly conduct a core seminar in which they and the students view the subject matter of the courses from their distinctive disciplinary, epistemological, and individual perspectives. A seventh teacher, called a "master learner," leads a linking seminar that has no independent content but seeks to help students integrate materials from the courses; and this teacher attends the six courses in which the students are enrolled.[9]

There are other approaches we can use to help students explore interconnections across courses and disciplines. We suggest, for example, an expanded use of linking seminars having no independent content but linking two or more courses that students are currently taking and that cluster around related issues or common themes. The function of these seminars is to explore with the students not just interrelations of the subject matters but the new knowledge that emerges as one looks at the problems on the basis of how they are treated in several disciplines. The introduction of a number of such seminars would reduce the number of traditional courses, but it would be an exciting step of bringing about curricular coherence among these offerings.

At the upper-division level, these seminars could provide students with an opportunity to reflect and analyze experiences and ideas that may not otherwise reach articulate consciousness. At this point in their careers, students are able to approach a wider variety of subject matters with an enlarged capacity for comprehension and for seeing connections and differences. They have been exposed to many subjects, and some have traveled, undertaken field research, or worked at paying jobs in which they have encountered many people, practices, structures, and organizations unrelated to academia. In a linking seminar, students can use this experience to reflect on the methodology and epistemology of their major, what related disciplines attempt to do, how they are doing it, and how well. Unlike traditional capstone courses, which tend to be global in nature and deal with topics of vast comprehensiveness—and may be resented by upperclass students preoccupied with their major—these seminars would focus on issues and themes related to their major.

Teaching linking seminars also brings great intellectual rewards to professors. Working on the connections across fields or topics helps faculty articulate the nature and the purpose of nonspecialized knowledge as well as teach it more effectively. Teaching a linking seminar once every two or three years can provide a freshness of approach to the professor's work while minimizing disruption of other teaching tasks. Although it takes intellectual courage to go beyond the security of a carefully honed disciplinary identity, professors who have taught in such interdisciplinary contexts report not just an enlargement of their scope of thinking but also a fresh impetus in the ways they approach problems in their own discipline.

REORIENTING TEACHING

ENCOURAGING ACTIVE LEARNING
ASSESSING STUDENT PROGRESS
ENLISTING STUDENTS AS COINQUIRERS
A NEW DEFINITION OF TEACHING

When we as faculty are asked about our courses, the questions tend to concern the topics we cover and the readings we assign rather than our teaching. Yet our style of interacting with our students, the methods we use to assure that they understand what we are trying to convey, and students' engagement in learning can spell the difference between success and failure in our goals for the course and for general education at large.

Students are not likely to develop a taste for ideas if they see thinking as an alien exercise that we demand of them and not as a pursuit that engages their own motivation and enlivens it with some passion. If we institute an ambitious new general education program without making clear to them its objective and principles, they are likely to resist it because it seems to interfere with their free choice, their interest in their major, and their anticipation of the things they need to know for their future careers or lifestyles. To win them to the realization that general education is more than a requirement "to be gotten out of the way," they need to see its relevance for their future beyond their transcripts.

All too often, our operational assumption as teachers is that learning takes place when we talk. But students learn when they talk to themselves and to others. What we say is filtered through their capacities and reinterpreted in terms that draw on their own prior learning. Cognitive research shows that when students have no framework to help make sense of new information,

The sort of teaching we propose requires that we encourage active learning and that we become knowledgeable about the ways in which our students hear, understand, interpret, and integrate ideas

---

much of what they hear is lost.[10] All of us know professors who present their subject matter in respectable ways but who fail to communicate it to students. Lectures that are clear, concise, and challenging to the tutored mind may lose the students listening to them. Roland Christensen of Harvard notes that traditional teaching is "like dropping ideas into the letter box of the subconscious. You know when they are posted, but you never know when they will be received or in what form."[11]

The sort of teaching we propose requires that we encourage active learning and that we become knowledgeable about the ways in which our students hear, understand, interpret, and integrate ideas. To do so, we must become observers of our students' ways of learning and we should seek to have them become coinquirers with us regarding their learning.

ENCOURAGING
ACTIVE LEARNING

How can the questions our courses raise become our student's own questions? A variety of methods, already practiced in some places, could become common practice in transforming students from passive listeners to active thinkers:

□ *Stimulating active comprehension.* Some teachers ask their students to write down in class their summary

and interpretation of a reading assignment or of the teacher's presentation. Such writing facilitates disciplined thinking and helps students discover gaps and insufficiencies in their reasoning as well as in that of the author or the instructor.

Another practice is to experiment with different ways of ending a class session. At the end of a lecture or a seminar, many faculty tend to summarize the main points of the session. If students write their own summaries, their grasp of what went on is considerably enhanced; and if they at times also hand in these summaries, teachers can obtain valuable information about how what they said was heard.

A teacher can occasionally leave the class for fifteen or thirty minutes and ask the students to carry on the thinking of the course by talking to each other or by writing their thoughts down. The teacher can then review with the class the kinds of issues that emerged and the implications of those issues for the students' interpretation of the course content.

□ *Students and faculty listening to each other.* Communication is difficult even in relatively small classes because students and professors often have not cultivated good listening habits and do not know how to be interactive. Genuine discussion is neither an amorphous voicing of opinions (at times below the level of bull sessions to which students bring at least genuine involvement in the topic) nor an orchestrated performance in which students behave like mindreaders trying to find their lines in the prearranged script of the professor.

Consider the problems evident in the following interchange during the fifth week of a class on economic theories.

Professor: Would someone please explain dual labor market theory?
Carol: Well, it's because women are always low paid...
Professor: Hmmm ... Tom, you try.
Tom: Well, in the nineteenth century, the country started to industrialize and ...
Professor: Let me stop you there, OK? That's history. Dual labor market theory postulates ...

The discontinuity between this professor's question and the students' answers—the unfinished phrases, the interruptions—raises doubts about whether the professor and students speak the same language and read the same texts. The professor's question sounds straightforward enough. The students should know that the word *explain* means to make an idea clear and intelligible, to talk about its parts. And since this is the fifth week of class, the student should know what *theory* is. But when Carol answers, she behaves as if the question were something like, "Why are women in the secondary labor market?" She gives not an explanation but a

"right" answer—the kind that would be appropriate in a multiple-choice test.

The professor does not want to discourage Carol or make her feel stupid, and so instead of saying, "You're wrong," or "I don't understand," or "Go on a little further," he mumbles "Hmmm" and moves on to Tom, leaving Carol puzzled. He deals more firmly with Tom, stopping him, and labeling his answer as "history," but Tom, who may have been providing a context for further remarks, gets no help in understanding the difference between history and theory as categories, nor does he even get a chance to complete his sentence as one would in ordinary polite conversation.

Why does this happen? It is unlikely that Carol and Tom are too intellectually immature and too unaccustomed to academic thinking to deal with certain kinds of questions. Instead, the professor and students have not agreed on a common vocabulary of inquiry. The professor has not permitted students to work from the knowledge about which they feel most confident—their own past thinking, life, and experience—and the class has not established practices that will facilitate the hard work of learning.

To have an effective discussion, instructors must be attentive to the quality of student reasoning and must ascertain the context of students' thought and the logic of their errors, rather than offering either unclear criticism, as here, that leaves students puzzled and ultimately feeling rejected or, at the opposite extreme, indiscriminate agreement and support. If faculty members use some of the strategies suggested above to gather evidence of the students' interpretation of course issues, they will find it easier to put specific comments in a larger context, and to respond to answers in ways that support the students' learning.

□ *Collaborative learning.* Collaboration both encourages active learning and helps faculty understand their students' ways of thinking about a problem. Some faculty members who use this approach find it helpful to divide their classes occasionally into small groups of perhaps four or five so that all students have a chance to articulate their views and can get reactions to them.

The following practice, suggested by Professors Donald Finkel and Stephen Monk of Evergreen State College and the University of Washington, respectively, illustrates the transformation of the teacher into one who observes and facilitates student learning. The professor walks into the class and hands out to every student a worksheet containing important questions and examples about the course material, along with instructions to form groups of five to discuss them. The students reassemble in groups and begin to discuss the questions on the sheet. After a few minutes, the professor joins one group, quietly watches and listens, but does not talk. After listening to the discussion, the professor suggests to group members that they are not getting anywhere because they misunderstood the example given in the first question. The professor tells them to draw out in pictures what the example describes, and as they do so, makes clarifying comments. The professor listens as discussion resumes, then moves to another group.

Keeping a class of students actively involved with course material with a minimum of direct support from the teacher requires an artfully written set of instructions and questions. Professors put their expert knowledge, their most provocative questions, and their insights about how students comprehend the material into the worksheets.[12]

Many instructors are reluctant to encourage learning in groups or teams. Yet we know through research and experience that many intellectual and other accomplishments are brought about by teams. Teamwork has obvious implications for deepening the capacity for relationship, friendship, and collaborative citizenship. It can lead students of different ethnic backgrounds and of different personalities not only to understand but fruitfully to work and live with each other.

Teachers will adapt such techniques

as we have mentioned to their own style of enabling students to learn. But the crux is to provide opportunities for their students to take the initiative to formulate and test their own ideas. Other techniques that encourage active involvement with course materials include:

□ *Using electronic media.* The expanding world of computers, interactive video, telecommunications, and information storage and retrieval can help faculty exercise ingenuity and imagination in encouraging students' participation. Studies of interactive video instruction in the laboratory sciences indicate that conceptual learning is much improved over that in traditional laboratory settings. The utility of television has been shown in teaching about the Vietnam War or the history of America's civil rights movement. And satellite hookups can connect classrooms across the country with eminent authors and scientists for dialogue through interactive video.

□ *Providing laboratory experiences without laboratories.* The natural sciences are laboratory disciplines in which truths are established and verified by laboratory measurement. Nevertheless, to offer a laboratory experience in general education science courses at many institutions, whether community colleges or large research universities, may be impractical because of limited finances or facili-

ties. Two alternative approaches have worked well in stimulating lab work.

The first of these involves extensive demonstrations in the lecture room. These demonstrations have long been a mainstay of classes for chemistry and physics majors, and some institutions have successfully used them in nonscientist's courses as well. Properly devised demonstrations can both pique student interest (as is evident from student course evaluations that praise them) and make conceptual developments very concrete—as by showing the nylon polymer form or seeing the bullet's momentum transferred to the ballistic pendulum.

A second promising alternative—a two-semester course on "The Theory and Practice of Science"—has been successfully developed at Columbia University and involves a modification of the "great books" approach long used at St. John's College. It begins by introducing the students to just enough mathematics to make scientific papers useful as a basis for study. The rest of the course is then devoted to reading sets of original scientific papers and tracing the development of sets of important concepts and developments. For example, the genetics section of the course reads original papers from Mendel's "Experiments in Plant Hybridization" to Watson's and Crick's work on DNA. The advantages of such a course include the freshness that comes from using original sources, flexibility in scheduling and pacing free of the physical constraints of a laboratory, appreciation for the historical and social contexts in which scientific research is carried out, balance between conceptual advances and laboratory development, a feeling of comfort for nonscientists in using printed materials, and creative forms of evaluations, such as examinations in which students analyze scientific articles from current journals. The course also has the special advantage of dealing with the frontiers of knowledge, superb research at the highest level, and the writings of seminal investigators, rather than the jejune level of many science texts.

☐ *Fostering out-of-classroom learning.* Definition of the faculty role in teaching and learning has traditionally centered on the classroom. But there are many ways to link the classroom with students' out-of-class lives, including fieldwork, tutoring, service projects, and cooperative education. In engineering, industrial internships have had a long and distinguished history. More recently the experiential learning movement has provided many other examples of extending education into the world beyond the campus. If off-campus experiences involve intellectual exploration, their meaning and that of in-class learning can be considerably enhanced.

One English professor has his poetry students teach poetry in local high schools, thereby enlivening the classroom through task-oriented service to others. M.I.T.'s University Research Opportunities Program, a pioneering and successful venture now more than ten years old, places students in research settings outside the formal course structure. Ernest Lynton has called on liberal arts faculty to demonstrate the relations of their disciplines to the external world through joint ventures and greater cooperation with business in order to reduce narrowness and fragmentation of curricula and help students develop competencies for reflective practice.[13] All faculty can think of ways in which student learning can take place outside of class while providing for classroom analysis and reflection on these experiences. Implementing these ideas will likely require overcoming some ingrained skepticism. It will also involve rethinking the faculty "load" and the course and credit system, perhaps even modifying our concept of what a course is and what activities deserve credit. But out-of-classroom learning experiments should be tested by their intellectual outcomes for students rather than by their unconventionality.

☐ *Encouraging student reflection on work.* Much student time is taken up by paid jobs, yet explorations of student work experiences have rarely been the focus of classroom activities.

Students often participate in work activities passively, without reflecting on them analytically or in depth. Even when their jobs are humdrum and menial, they offer a context for understanding and can become a source for learning.

Colleges and universities can help students develop frameworks for examining the culture of their work settings. Classroom investigation of students' employment can concern itself not only with the location and function of their jobs in the industrial and commercial order but also with such aspects as relationships with other workers, supervisors, customers, and clients. As an illustration, Hamline University has developed an internship program for its students who receive pay for their work whenever possible, and it has created courses to relate the liberal arts to the workplace. Thus in "The Workplace: Experience and Reflection," humanities students explore the ethical, aesthetic, and historical aspects of work as revealed in humanities literature. Similar courses are available to students in such fields as psychology and social work.

□ *Using undergraduates as teaching assistants.* Employing undergraduates as teaching assistants can be a powerful device for enchancing their learning. Faculty who have tried it—and there are more than is commonly realized—have usually been enthusias-

tic. Undergraduate T.A.s learn much about their subject matter because they need to engage in thinking through the materials of the course. In addition, the students whom they draw into reflection and discussion show enhanced understanding and motivation for the course. Particularly in institutions in which large classes are common, the use of undergraduate teaching assistants makes possible the creation of that small group interaction which is especially conducive to active learning.

At Brown, undergraduates who are nominated by faculty serve as Writing Fellows to help integrate the study of writing into a wide variety of courses throughout the curriculum. Each student in these courses is assigned to a Writing Fellow who evaluates the strengths and weaknesses of the students' papers and makes constructive suggestions for improving them. Students then revise their work and submit both versions (the one with the fellow's comments and the revision) to their teaching assistant or professor. Students meet with their Writing Fellow at least once a semester for an individual conference. Institutions that employ undergraduates in such roles could award these students academic credit for learning connected with their work through, for example, a seminar on "The Theory and Teaching of Writing," for which the teaching of writing serves as a practicum.

□ *Promoting undergraduate research.* At various times over the past decades, American students have taken the initiative in their own education, as in the "free universities" of the late 1960s. On some campuses, students have initiated their own research enterprises, such as Stanford's Student Workshops on Psychological and Social Issues (SWOPSI). Student-initiated research, enlisting faculty in the consultant role, is a wonderful way to have students discover research competencies on their own, as in fact they can best be discovered. Through exercise, trial, and error, what students learn becomes naturally their own mental equipment. Experience shows that when students confront real problems in research or in other activities, they much more avidly turn to experienced elders for help than they do in the classroom.

While undergraduates can undertake research on many topics, they are particularly well suited to conducting research on the academic and nonacademic life of their own institutions. Undergraduate research courses devoted to studying various aspects of academic programs, student life, and administrative arrangements can provide valuable data and also be a stimulus for reform. In the few places in which they have been tried, such courses have worked well. Courses in the social sciences, including method-

ology courses, lend themselves naturally to this purpose, but courses in other fields can serve as well. They give students an opportunity to articulate and understand processes that go on under their eyes but that otherwise may not reach their consciousness.

□ *Collaborative course development.* Collaborative development of courses is another promising educational experiment. Students are drawn into working relationships with peers and with faculty, replacing the traditional didactic modes of the classroom. For example, at Ohio University, faculty members who plan to offer new interdisciplinary courses draw on a panel of other faculty, students, alumni, and invited guests in a five-week seminar to assist in the planning of the courses and their syllabi. At the State University of New York at Oswego, groups of faculty and students working together over the year develop new interdisciplinary courses on topics of ethical and cultural importance such as "Tolerance and Prejudice," and "Myth and Symbol." At Brown University, student observers of courses provide feedback to faculty members for possible revisions of both course content and pedagogy; in its Odyssey program, pairs of students and faculty either create new courses in response to contemporary issues or newly emerging areas of inquiry, or develop new components for existing courses, such as a segment on

environmental issues for an economics course.[14]

These teaching approaches make
use of group efforts, of student-
student and of student-teacher collaboration. We believe there are
significant benefits to the quality of
learning when faculty members encourage collaborative learning. In addition, asking students to participate
with others in defining, framing, and
arguing problems prepares them for a
time when the quality of their work
may depend on their ability to
engage in collaboration with others.
Recent descriptions of college
students have berated their self-
centeredness and even narcissism. Yet
our educational institutions encourage
many campus practices that make
learning a private activity. For evaluation, undergraduates face their instructor alone; and the award of the
grade can be one of lonely splendor
or disappointment. This centering of
learning in the individual may limit
both learning and action. At the
same time, many students are dis-
posed to conform unnecessarily to
group norms and to adopt conventional views, attitudes, and stereotypes without reflection. Thus both
self-centeredness and conformity limit
students' learning.

ASSESSING STUDENT PROGRESS

As teachers, we have several assessment tools at our disposal. Foremost
are the tests we administer to our
students. Reading final exams can be
a humbling experience in seeing what
our students have not learned—and
how much they may have misunderstood or distorted our ideas.

We assess classroom performance
through grades, although many of us
have at least some doubts about the
validity of the grades we give. For instance, when teachers are asked to
nominate intellectually creative
students in their fields, they do not
necessarily choose those to whom
they give A's. In addition, some goals
of general education do not lend
themselves to conventional letter
grades and may require fresh
evaluative criteria and techniques,
such as the use of portfolios and nar-
rative transcripts.

A third tool is student evaluations
of our teaching. Unfortunately, most
evaluations give far too few details
about teaching processes. Most of
them, moreover, are made at the end
of the term when they can no longer
affect the outcome of the course,
rather than during the course, when
they could guide its progress.

Apart from these techniques, we
rarely take an investigative look at
our teaching or at its impact on our
students. Audiotaping and videotap-

When students are no longer treated
as objects of our plans
but are instead enlisted as coinquirers,
they develop levels of reflectiveness
and maturity that are surprising

ing of class sessions can provide valuable data, but they are rarely exploited in a sophisticated way. In planning and rethinking our courses, we need to gather more ample data and develop our skills of interpreting them. Do students learn what we teach? Do they study what we assign and benefit from it, or are they turned off by it? How can we reach more of them?

It would be curious if teaching were the only profession not in need of an underlying theory and of continuing inquiry; yet something like this is expressed in the not uncommon self-perception of faculty as having arrived at the permanent stage of "good teacher." The task group believes that assessment is an indispensable tool for conducting and improving courses, and hence we hold that assessing their courses ought to be a regular task of all instructors and be undertaken while their courses are in progress. Without continuing and well-designed assessments that illuminate the what and how of learning as evidenced in the day-by-day activities of students, courses are deprived of their essential rudder. Good assessment is not just a summary good or bad grade or an index of satisfactions. It is a prime tool for the continuing vitality and continual redefinition of courses in the light of evaluated experience.

One approach to course assess-

ment, recently tested in several institutions, provides an example of inquiry into teaching.[15] It involves two faculty members collaborating with each other over a semester or longer. One of them teaches her or his class, and the other observes the class approximately once a week. Both the teacher and the observer regularly interview a small number of students from the class in order to ascertain the learning styles, methods, and progress of the students. The teacher and the observer meet about once a week to reflect on their observations and interviews and to refine their skills of articulating how students learn. They also collect documents from their students, such as notes taken during class, and they scrutinize exams and essays with attention not only to content but also to the learning skills and cognitive schemes by which the students approach course contents. Further understanding of the ways in which students learn comes from periodic class sessions in which the students together with the teacher examine the methods and processes by which knowledge in the subject matter is acquired, including the epistemological underpinnings of the discipline. These observations and analyses can quickly lead to experimentation that in turn leads to further inquiry.

After teaching and being observed for a term or more, the professor observes another colleague's course, gaining further perspective upon his or her teaching and that of others. If groups of faculty meet to analyze student learning on the basis of examples drawn from the classroom by videotape or other means, sophistication and depth of assessment can be further enhanced.

ENLISTING STUDENTS AS COINQUIRERS

Even more important than the involvement of our faculty colleagues in assessment is the involvement of our students. Obtaining sustained feedback from them as coinquirers into both the substance and the procedures of learning may be the single most important ingredient not only for transforming our teaching but increasing students' learning. We have found again and again that when students are no longer treated as objects of our plans but are instead enlisted as coinquirers, they develop levels of reflectiveness and maturity that are surprising when we know them only from their usual behavior in the classroom and their term papers and examinations.

The procedures we advocate aim at enhancing student reflectiveness about their own learning. Their thinking will progress better if they become aware of how they think. Recent learning theory has begun to suggest that sophistication about the how of learning greatly enhances one's learning capacities.[16] When students are aware of what they are doing, they can more deliberately adopt effective methods of learning and gain a deeper sense of what the objectives and significance of inquiries are. Epistemological inquiry thus ought to be part of many courses, including general education courses.

□ One such technique can take the form of an intellectual diary in two columns with students noting in one column what they are learning and in the other how they go about it and what they think to be the significance of what they are learning.

□ Even modest efforts, such as asking students during a class session to reflect in writing for ten or fifteen minutes on what they are learning in the course and how they are learning it, can be very instructive. By asking students to do this even just a few times during a term, we can gain valuable information that we can use later in the term.

□ More extensive methods of assessment include analytic sessions with all or some of the students in one's class, involving exploration of the processes and effects of the course on their learning and the review of portfolios that demonstrate their competencies through their products. These methods not only enhance our knowledge of student achievement but also provide students with valuable tools of self-assessment.

☐ We might invite some or all of the students in a course to respond to a learning-styles inventory.[17] Such inventories can provide information on the degree of individuals' analytic, logical-deductive, reflective, intuitive, aesthetic, imaginative, synthesizing, and generalizing approaches to learning. All of us clearly differ in our intellectual propensities and abilities, showing varying strengths in logical, mathematical, intuitive, spatial, aesthetic, and interpersonal forms of thinking, just as do lawyers, physicists, political leaders, architects, poets, and psychiatrists. While knowledge of learning styles is at an early stage both at the practical and the theoretical levels, our awareness of how students go about learning and our responsiveness to their particular learning styles seems critical in increasing their learning.

Confronting our own individual cognitive styles and those of our students can be surprising and revealing. We may not have been aware that we have a distinctive learning style. We almost immediately come to see that some of the problems we have had with some or many of our students are because our styles do not mesh with theirs. Faculty who examine differences among their students' learning styles frequently begin to explore how they can develop ap-

proaches appropriate to a broad range of students' learning styles and strategies.

Students of human development have shown us that teachers are heard differently by students at varying stages of their cognitive development, and they have given us some road maps to identify phases of growth. In addition to Piaget and Perry, we have the writings of such people as Astin, Belenky and her associates, Chickering, Freedman, Sanford, and Shaughnessy.[18] We have a beginning investigation of differences of "frames of mind" in the research of such people as Howard Gardner.[19] We ignore such writers at the peril of not hearing what our students tell us in their own ways.

Naturally we need to guard against the dangers of relying too narrowly on any descriptive scheme of student thinking and of stereotyping students who in different courses may exhibit different intellectual capacities or "phases" of development. But we can use available descriptions as starting points for our own thinking, and we can become our own investigators by making our own observations and discoveries in the classroom about our students' ways of thinking. Knowledge of student learning should not be the province of cognitive psychologists alone but instead should belong to all faculty members and students, since their interaction hinges on it. If we enlist our students as collaborators in the learning process, their efforts at self-awareness will enrich both our teaching and their own learning.

A NEW DEFINITION
OF TEACHING

We are doing more than suggesting useful techniques for teaching. We are proposing a shift in the definition of teaching. We propose approaches that make it possible for us to find out not just what our students learn but how they learn it and what motivates them. Informing students about the purposes of our courses and programs, obtaining sophisticated feedback from them, and collaborating with them are indispensable activities under this expanded definition of teaching. Our inquiry becomes considerably richer if we shift attention from measuring student "satisfaction" with our courses, even if high, to what students learn from them. Once our focus is upon what students learn and how they go about learning, our emphasis can shift to exploration and experimentation. A host of fresh pedagogic techniques can emerge once we know more about how our students perceive what we say and what mental and emotional efforts they must make to grasp the materials of our courses.

The rewards of this approach are great. Seeking knowledge about student learning opens up a fresh field for faculty investigation. It greatly increases our communication with students, and their responsiveness turns teaching into a more satisfying experience for us, as we are relieved of the debilitating sense of dragging our students into a direction they do not want to go. We can renew our intellectual vitality from the intellectual participation of our students and gain a new sense of pedagogic satisfaction from fostering their growth.

A recent report on medical education from the Association of American Medical Colleges is relevant to this new approach to teaching. It makes five primary suggestions:
□ considerable reduction of reliance on memorizing,
□ identification of the major concepts or principles in the areas under study,
□ emphasis on students' independent learning that carries over into postschool lives,
□ reduction of lecturing, and
□ replacement of lecturing by small group instruction.[20]
These changes in teaching proposed by medical educators are equally important outside of medical education. They have particular relevance to the teaching of general education, with its emphasis on encouraging life-long independent learning.

ASSURING INSTITUTIONAL SUPPORT

CHANGING THE ENVIRONMENT
INTEGRATING COMMUTER STUDENTS
IMPROVING RESIDENTIAL LIFE
EXPANDING CROSS-CULTURAL EXPERIENCES
CREATING CROSS-DISCIPLINARY SEMINARS
ORGANIZING CAMPUS THINK TANKS
ASSESSING PROGRAMS
ASSURING ADMINISTRATIVE SUPPORT
REVITALIZING GENERAL EDUCATION

All too frequently our institutions develop general education programs and overlook significant details. For instance, we may draft elaborate objectives such as helping students to think critically while overlooking the basic fact that they may often come to class without even having read the assignment. This fact overshadows much else and can defeat our efforts as instructors before we enter the classroom. Attention to it calls for collaboration among faculty and with administrators and students because no single instructor can easily go against established institutional norms. It calls for sustained explorations with students of what their part of the educational "contract" is.

CHANGING THE ENVIRONMENT

General education has to confront the existence of two cultures in academia: that of faculty and that of students. On many campuses, students

We suggest that catalogues show graphically and intelligibly how courses from different disciplines can easily be grouped around a selection of common themes

view faculty with the ambivalence of respect and resentment, admiration and disappointment. Depending on the institution and the department, relations between students and faculty can range from harmony and colleagueship through mutual avoidance to antagonism and undeclared conflict. On such campuses, the rhetoric about an "intellectual community" is belied by the reality of these two separate cultures.

The significance for student learning of such environmental factors has long been recognized. Research indicates the importance of students' relationships with their own peers, the nature of residential life and of recreational and leisure facilities, and such difficult-to-formulate yet very potent factors as institutional ethos and self-definition for shaping students' college careers and intellectual development.[21] Faculty who have engaged in this research or read about it have generally been humbled to see the relatively small role that the classroom and their teaching play in this process. The correspondingly large role of the environment outside of the classroom is particularly salient for general education, which focuses on the development of the whole person: attitudes of character as well as intellectual skills and knowledge.

How can we begin to change these environmental factors in order to encourage general education? An obvious starting point is the college catalogue, which seldom makes clear the thinking and competency that general education calls for. Only a knowledgeable examination of its pages can identify implicit possibilities: courses that cluster around important issues or themes that transcend disciplinary and departmental boundaries— be they the evolution of political and societal forms, the policy implications of human inventions in thought or technology, the harmony and disharmony of cultures, or the worldwide problems of poverty and malnutrition. We suggest that catalogues show graphically and intelligibly how courses from different disciplines can easily be grouped around a selection of common themes. As students seek to design their own programs of study, their planning can be greatly assisted by a scheme of listings oriented to these common themes.

A second way of changing institutional practices to support general education is to combine freshman orientation with introductory courses. Orientation is often confined to the first few days of the year—a time when most beginning students are bewildered, anxious, and preoccupied with issues more immediate than the vistas opening to them in their initial courses. Orientation ought to span the first half, if not the entire length, of the freshman year. A number of institutions have done this by integrating traditional orientation activities and advising with first-year courses required of all students. Emory University, for example, has recently experimented with a seminar that introduces beginning students to selected books, musical compositions, and other works of art. The faculty are knowledgeable amateurs rather than experts in most areas of this course, and they join the students in a variety of activities, including listening to the music and going to concerts and art exhibits. Through this approach, they seek to provide a personal orientation to the academic life of the campus and help students see the interconnections between the classroom and the world from which the classroom derives its contents.

Perhaps the most urgent reform on most campuses in improving general education involves academic advising. To have programs and courses become coherent and significant to students requires adequate advising; yet observers frequently report that such advising is unavailable. On many campuses, advising consists of perfunctory faculty approval of student course schedules. On others, it consists of staff guidance regarding graduation requirements and course prerequisites. On still others, computers now provide basic directions and warnings.

Student conversations mirror the jumble evident on many a transcript:

□ "I wanted to take 10-B this fall so I could get into 116 next year, but the only section I could fit into my schedule was filled; so I'm going to take 7-A and get that out of the way instead."

□ "Did you know that you could substitute 24-C for 22-D and count it toward your natural science requirement? Freshmen can take it with permission of the instructor. That's where all the phys. ed. majors go."[22]

Even if we as faculty wish we could devote more time to advising, many of us have not quite mastered its art. We practice advising as a form of telling and feel the compulsion to make authoritative statements beyond our knowledge and experience, rather than concentrating on listening and enabling the students to explore and make their own decisions. Individual advising is particularly demanding upon our time, yet few of us have tried to organize group advising. Group advising can save much time, particularly in regard to issues that are repeated from student to student and may just as well be treated at one time. Moreover, the group has special potency to combine information dissemination with student-faculty exploration of educational issues and with the development of student reliance on and augmentation of their own resources and capacities.

One effective approach to freshmen advising involves a faculty adviser meeting regularly with a group of about ten or fifteen freshmen, perhaps once a week early in the year and less often thereafter. Associated with the group can be one or two junior or senior students knowledgeable about the institution and its requirements. The time saved by avoiding the repetition of information to each student separately allows the professor to seek out students individually and be sought out by them for those issues and problems that are best handled on a one-to-one basis. Wherever the information of the professor and upperclass students is limited, such as about prerequisites or the content of certain courses or programs, one or two members of the group working as a team can be asked to seek the particular facts and report back to the group. Academic questions can lead to a discussion of students' campus experiences, attitudes, goals, and difficulties. After an initial period, advisees can meet periodically without the professor in order to develop their own autonomy, but the professor's periodic involvement with the group as students pass through the college years can provide them with a source of continuing personal counsel.

Such group advising might seem to reduce the already tenuous individual contact between students and faculty, especially at large universities. Nonetheless, we believe that good group advising is better than perfunctory individual advising. Moreover, in this proposed scheme, individual advising sessions can become special occasions to focus on a student's unique problems and aspirations. An additional benefit stems from the participation of upper-division students in the advising process. They can play a nurturing role of big sister or brother; they develop closer colleagueship with their faculty mentor; and they become more invested in the institution itself.

The procedures suggested here are likely to lead not only to better advising but also to a deepening of our understanding of students' lives. This benefit extends beyond advising to our classes. An enhanced understanding of our students' cognitive and emotional dispositions can greatly influence the messages we convey, sometimes implicitly, even in large lecture classes. Students know whether we address them as individuals or only as some blurred multitude below the podium; and they respond with greatly increased motivation if they feel that we recognize their own strivings, problems, and successes.

Students' academic direction and vitality are inextricably bound up with their hopes, fears, and self-esteem. For us to leave the emotional side of students' personality untouched or relegated to other staff is to invite defeat for many of our educational objectives. Counselors and psychiatric staff can help students explore their attitudes and increase their motivation, and they can sensitize faculty to the emotional aspects of students' lives. But faculty members, both because of their sheer number and their influence over students' grades, are pivotal in communicating the message of the college. If we abandon everything but cerebral and classroom tasks, our students may never attain their intellectual potential. By our involvement in advising, we can respond to their needs without overstepping the boundaries of our own faculty expertise.

INTEGRATING
COMMUTER STUDENTS

The majority of the nation's college students do not live in college residences but instead are commuters. Life at home and at work may insulate them from the challenge and transforming power of a college education. Many of the procedures we have described earlier for linking classroom learning with outside activities are particularly relevant to commuting students. In fact, students' off-campus experiences offer special opportunities for reflection in the classroom. While residential students live in a relatively homogeneous environment, commuters live in and need to balance the worlds of school,

home, community, and work. Their employment can provide opportunities for intellectual explorations. Major questions in economics, sociology, political science, psychology, history, and other fields can and should be related to this intricate net of circumstances in which commuters are enmeshed; circumstances of which they may not otherwise become adequately aware and thus be deprived both of a major source of learning and an opportunity to take better control of their lives.

Many commuting students see their institution as a service station, and they may view its efforts to encourage their development as interference. Students hurrying from home to campus and then to work have few opportunities to sit down leisurely with peers and mull over interests generated in the classroom and in their lives. Yet we can take deliberate steps to compensate for the lack of institutional affiliation that commuting life entails. Institutions that operate student residences can offer commuters the opportunity of becoming affiliates of these residences. All institutions can seek space in public and other buildings near their commuting students' places of living and encourage activities that allow them to get together. Faculty can encourage classroom-based projects that link commuting students with each other and with residents. Faculty and administrators can facilitate exposure of commuters to events on and off campus, such as exhibits and movies, and to people, such as scholars, knowledgeable citizens, and alumni. Commuters can meet with faculty and other students at convenient off-campus sites. The simple experience of visiting different neighborhoods and meeting people from different backgrounds can greatly add to students' and faculty members' knowledge of and empathy with cultural diversity.

IMPROVING RESIDENTIAL LIFE

Residential arrangements within the college walls are potent factors in the educational process. These influences can be freeing or inhibiting. In many institutions, dormitory life is an anti-intellectual counterforce to the culture of the classroom. Often what takes place in the residence halls defeats the efforts of faculty to have students develop their skills of thoughtful reflection.

Campus residences represent society in miniature, albeit society uncharacteristic of usual American life with the exception of the armed services. Students are often mixed heterogeneously in close quarters and live in semi-community with each other in a setting quite different from the separated homes or apartments they may occupy for the rest of their lives.

Some observers have talked of the college years as a "moratorium" in which real life is suspended, giving young adults a chance to try out ways of living and thinking in relative protection from some of the exigencies of the external world. Residential life is in some ways a partial suspension of reality. But in other respects it is a replica of "real" life: in the friendships and conflicts growing out of intimate association, the competition and cooperation between individuals, the striving for status, and the political maneuvering of individuals and groups. All this is a rich source for reflection, study, and growth. Unfortunately, administrative divisions between student affairs and academic offices interfere with the integration of classroom and residential life. Close collaboration between student affairs and academic administrators is essential to this integration.

Among examples of such integration are "theme houses," in which an entire residence is given over to the pursuit of a particular topic, such as international relations, a foreign language and culture, the impact of science and technology upon society, the ethnological exploration of different societies, the study of an historical tradition, the production of plays, or social service. A faculty member interested in the theme typically serves as the director of such a residence and may live there with her or his family. These houses offer opportunities for much talk and other interaction between students and faculty. They further the development of students not only as individuals but also as social beings whose sociability includes considerable attention to intellect. Every residential college might give every student the opportunity to be, for at least one year, a member of such a group.

Theme houses and ordinary residences can be strengthened by affiliating with them not only faculty and staff but also people from the community. Affiliated community members can provide students with examples of mature intellectuality that extend beyond the areas in which their professors have expertise. Many effective people in the community outside the college have great interest in being close to students, but colleges rarely take initiative to seek them out. Affiliates may be given an honorific title, such as Fellow or Mentor. They will not only come to the campus but also invite students into their homes and introduce them to their community, business, or professional associates and activities, thus strengthening the students' sense of the world beyond the campus.

On some campuses, such changes in residential life must proceed carefully. Students tend to regard the residences as their turf, and they may resent well-meaning attempts at inte-

gration, such as holding classes in them, as an invasion of their privacy. Their resentment is a symptom that they make a division between their own life and that of the classroom, and it indicates a problem to be overcome rather than an attitude to be accepted at face value. Association between faculty and students around their mutual professional and other interests can help overcome this division.

EXPANDING CROSS-CULTURAL EXPERIENCES

Learning to establish fruitful associations with students who are culturally and psychologically different from oneself is an endeavor made imperative by the greatly changing ethnic composition of this country and the continuing internationalization of Americans' interests and concerns. Foreign travel is not the only means for broadening perspectives. Faculty and students in many areas of the country can find culturally diverse groups very near their campuses, and many unused opportunities exist near home for intercultural acquaintance and understanding.

A long-term program devoted to world interdependence at Wheaton College in Massachusetts began with the idea that the way to increase student awareness of diversity is to start with the faculty. The program thus has an immediate effect on the cur-

We need institutional arrangements
that make it possible for faculty
to adopt roles and develop competencies
that go beyond our own highly
developed disciplinary ways of thinking

riculum. During January terms and summers, faculty spend from four to eight weeks living and working in non-Western societies about which they have little previous knowledge. They go not as experts to familiar places but as learners to new environments such as Kenya, Korea, Thailand, Egypt, Israel, and the Seychelles. The intent is that the teachers incorporate relevant texts and ideas from countries they visit into their core curriculum courses, rather than leave them to specialized courses that might be taken by only a few students. The program provides an environment in which international students also become a resource in conjunction with faculty who have been to their countries, thus strengthening the global perspective for all students. Wheaton is now planning the second phase of its program, which will enable all students to have a study experience abroad before they graduate.

Closer to home, cross-cultural experiences can also involve crossing the cultural boundaries of academic disciplines. A simple way of encouraging the general education of faculty is to encourage them to take courses given by their colleagues. This has been an occasional practice of some faculty who are willing to play the learning role and take their colleagues' courses not so much for the sake of advancement in their own discipline as for the intellectual pleasure of increasing their general knowledge. Their experience allows them to have a more empathic view of the challenges and problems that their students confront in learning. Moreover, when students see faculty members as colearners in their courses, their view of the significance of these courses increases immeasurably.

CREATING CROSS-DISCIPLINARY SEMINARS

One major obstacle to making general education work is the attempt to offer general education through a conglomerate of courses conceived along specialized disciplinary lines. The problem is that most of us who teach undergraduates do not ourselves engage in the sort of integrative learning across fields we expect of our students. We need institutional arrangements that make it possible for faculty to adopt roles and develop competencies that go beyond our own highly developed disciplinary ways of thinking.

Cross-disciplinary seminars for faculty members are one means of encouraging them to think about broader contexts for their particular research and teaching interests. Cross-disciplinary seminars bring together a group of instructors who teach courses which have related topics and themes. When these instructors meet, all the participants are amateurs about the theme except in the areas pertaining to their own discipline. This can at first be bewildering. Some may assert imperiously that their own fields hold a privileged perspective on the common problem. But the more often such a group meets, the more its members realize how the problem is illuminated from several perspectives and how one disciplinary approach is more or less subtly challenged and enriched through exposure to others.

If such cross-disciplinary seminars are to prosper, they must draw on the intellectual interests and expertise that led individual faculty members to design their particular courses in the first place. By appealing to that interest, the seminars can reasonably expect that the faculty participants will be willing to meet at agreed-upon intervals to discuss the perspectives of their disciplines in regard to a common problem that cuts across their several courses. Because such seminars appeal to the intellectual and disciplinary interests of faculty members, it is more likely that faculty members will join willingly, even enthusiastically. Their appetite for cross-disciplinary exploration is likely to grow through the experience. Some universities have institutionalized such talk across the disciplines in terms of faculty research interests. Columbia's University Seminars are one example of long standing. The University of Chicago and Stanford University have long offered cross-disciplinary seminars for faculty members from liberal arts colleges in their region and have found that interest in participating in these seminars has grown steadily through the years.

These cross-disciplinary seminars may involve only faculty. But when faculty organize seminars which include undergraduates, the impact on the students is strong. The students encounter multiple approaches to learning and they experience the potentially productive anxiety that comes from recognizing the uncertainty of knowledge. Such anxiety is a means of leading students to explore the nature of knowledge and their own role in acquiring it.

ORGANIZING CAMPUS THINK TANKS

The methods of inquiry we have developed in the academy should be applied to the work of the academy itself. Beyond cross-disciplinary seminars for faculty, we propose the creation of institutional think tanks to treat problems in general education as intellectual issues before they solidify into political ones.

Perhaps the best resource for implementing some of the ideas presented in this report is the available faculty talent for curricular and teaching change. As surveys have shown, a large proportion of faculty are willing to engage in curricular or teaching experimentation. The problem is that they often feel isolated, and adequate structures through which they can express their experimental bent rarely exist. These faculty must be identified and helped to affiliate with each other and with administrators in order to encourage their thinking and experimentation.

Both faculty members and administrators need to be more articulate about the educational process. We may talk about ideas in our discipline with great specificity, learning, and cogency, but we often resort to anecdotes when commenting upon the overall educational enterprise. We will tell how things were when we were undergraduates and describe, for instance, a professor who was tough but expected much of us, or a professor who was kindly at the right moment. Sometimes we make fantastic generalizations, such as that good students will learn from almost any teacher but that very little can help poor students. Such stereotypes underline the need for bringing our thinking about undergraduate education to a level of sophistication comparable to that within our disciplines.

Anthropologists, historians, sociologists, psychologists, and professors of literature should be encouraged to apply the tools of their disciplines to understanding the process of under-

graduate education. Through campus think tanks on the educational process, such faculty and administrators can bring a new articulateness to this process. The group can address itself to the question of its institution's definition of general education as practiced and not as stated in the catalogue. It can facilitate educational fact finding and theory building, seeking to determine, for instance, what competencies students in fact acquire—whether in languages, writing, or reasoning—and how they acquire them. It can take a leadership role in the continuing discussion about general education that we recommended in the first chapter and it can become an important instrument for faculty and administrative action in strengthening undergraduate education.

Administrative involvement is clearly necessary in this process. In the press of managerial tasks, the issues of education often suffer neglect. Think tank meetings could stimulate administrators' educational thinking and, by having a regular place on presidential and vice presidential schedules, provide an organizational base for sophisticated educational initiative. The ideas emanating from those interactions could inform the administrators' work and dialogue with faculty, other administrators, and trustees, enabling them to provide inspirational leadership on educational matters. Such ideas could affect their public pronouncements and help create a more enlightened climate of educational opinion in the public at large.

We believe that the reform of general education should not ordinarily be entrusted to the usual curriculum committee, whose normal business is to consider the courses that are recommended for inclusion among the institution's offerings. A more promising approach is to turn the task over to the members of the think tank. The attitude of the members of the group would be professorial: They would read, discuss, question guests, and write on the topic of general education at their institution. As they think about the issues, they would acquaint themselves with the ideas of their colleagues as well as with what is known about the kinds of effective teaching that lead to continued learning. They would come to a sophisticated awareness of the history of their own institution and of its capabilities for mounting different educational programs. They would become well acquainted with the students it has attracted and acquire some sense of the kind of students who are likely to be admitted in the foreseeable future.

This mix of specific empirical knowledge and more general normative discussions should, if things go well, generate some consensus if not a philosophy regarding general educa-

tion at the institution. When enough clarity has been achieved, the group could begin to produce occasional papers on aspects of general education. Such papers could be seen as local versions of national reports, which are inevitably too general and to various degrees inapplicable to specific situations. By confining their scope to the institution itself yet treating their topic within a national and historical context, the quality of general education will inevitably be improved.

Finally, to be effective, the group will need to arrange frequent and task-minded discussions of their documents with a large proportion of their colleagues. Unless other faculty and administrators undergo a process of thinking similar to that of the group, they are unlikely to understand and even less likely to agree with its recommendations. Miami University in Ohio offers a particularly successful example of such a process: Its current three-year reform effort at general education enlists in varying ways all segments of its community in the enterprise of deliberation and planning. Its effort is guided by a twenty-three member steering committee consisting of faculty, students, and administrators, while a smaller executive committee concentrates on policy issues and evaluates the overall process. Every department names a liaison to the steering committee, which uses a variety of chan-

We propose that when faculty
undertake educational planning
they talk with students and above all,
listen to them talk about their ambitions
and their experiences in the institution

---

nels to involve in the reform process the entire university community, including the campus newspaper, public meetings, and mailings to the entire faculty. Faculty members are encouraged to write comments and suggestions to the steering committee; these statements are distributed to all committee members and become a part of their work materials.

ASSESSING PROGRAMS

When general educational programs are planned, it is curious how little students are consulted or made a focus of observation in determining feasibility. To some extent the reason may stem from our ambivalence about student involvement, which in the 1960s took on strong political connotations and then seemed to subside in the 1970s, when student "apathy" reflected students' lack of interest in deliberations in which they did not have a truly participative voice or did not perceive as serving their needs. We propose that when faculty undertake educational planning they talk with students, observe them, use data about them— data often already available in various offices of their institution— and above all, listen to them talk about their ambitions and their experiences in the institution.

It would be ironic if institutions otherwise devoted to inquiry and dis-

covery failed to agree that in regard to the curriculum and teaching, inquiry and discovery are integral, normal activities. Regular evaluation of entire programs as well as individual courses is necessary to keep curriculum and teaching alive. Yet program evaluation or assessment seems to be an arcane art, forbidding to the uninitiated. When assessment is directed toward general education, it may seem even more mystifying because the program serves a multitude of purposes, many of them vaguely articulated. Thus some faculty and administrators renounce educational assessment, arguing that education is too ineffable to be subjected to measurement, that the ends of education cannot be specified with sufficient precision, or that assessment is inherently dehumanizing and mechanical.

The problem with this response is that it dismisses the power that a careful assessment can wield. The art of assessment is far from perfect, but it is a feasible art and can stimulate curiosity, foster self-consciousness, and strengthen education, particularly when it involves faculty and students who have a stake in what is being assessed. It shifts the ground of the discussion about general education from rhetoric and unsupported assertions to its actual consequences. It helps identify unanticipated problems with the implementation of a program and may suggest midcourse corrections while identifying unintended outcomes that may nevertheless be beneficial. It can serve political purposes, generating or retaining support for the program and describing it to prospective students and to alumni, trustees, foundation officials, and legislators.

Program assessments are frequently undertaken by external evaluators. While an external perspective can be useful, leadership and participation by those who carry out the program is critical in assuring that the results of the assessment will be heeded. Faculties can design their own evaluation procedures and, in collaboration with administrators and students, identify the questions that are most worth asking about their program and the kinds of actions such information may usefully support. Assigning responsibility to a faculty oversight committee to develop and approve a plan and designating the person or persons to administer the assessment can help assure that useful information is generated. Some resources of time and money are needed, but the process can be a low-cost, high-yield activity. The following six principles, which we offer as guidelines for a home-grown approach to assessment of a general education curriculum, can help assure its success:

□ Assessments are most useful when they are "formative" in nature, that is, when they entail observing the learning process and using the information that is generated to improve its effectiveness. There will come a time when it will be necessary to make summary statements and decisions, but assessment should be an aid to improvement based on the experience of participants, especially during the early phases of a program.

□ Assessment should be performed through the use of multiple methods. Questionnaire surveys, individual and group interviews, and tests all contribute to understanding the operations and consequences of an academic program; each is more convincing if coordinated with some other method.[23]

□ Similarly, assessment should include multiple sources of information. The director of a program may have one perspective, faculty members another, and the students yet a third.

□ Quantitative as well as qualitative information is needed. One must count participants, collect structured questionnaire data, indicate achievement levels, or otherwise have numbers to report, but it is equally necessary to give participants an opportunity to frame their own responses to the program and illustrate points with their individual observations of and experiences with courses and teachers. There is power in both numbers and perceptions.

□ The program as a whole and each of its major components should be assessed. Just as the program is more than the sum of its parts, so should the assessment be. Departmental boundaries and inadequate communication among departments make comprehensive assessment both challenging and essential.

□ Interpretation of the data will be more illuminating if they are viewed in relation to similar data from comparable campuses. A comparative approach involving several institutions can bring additional credibility to assessment, increase insights through different interpretations of the data, and forge stronger links among comparable institutions.

Utilizing the results is where many program evaluations break down. Reports are compiled, distributed, and filed, but then forgotten. The benefits of assessment—curiosity, self-awareness, improvement—can be realized only if individuals receive reliable information, reflect on its meanings, discuss its implications with others, and take actions based on the new perspectives. The best guarantee that results will be used is for those involved in the program to feel that the questions are *their* questions on issues of concern to them, answered in ways they understand and trust. Students, faculty, and administrators must be asked to identify the most pressing concerns, identify the questions to be asked, review the design, and make sure it has credibility with the relevant decision makers. They

must then discuss the results with an eye toward making changes. These discussions can take place in many different contexts, involving faculty and trustee committees, individual departments, and such administrative offices as admissions, development, and public information.

In starting a new educational program, a pilot phase is desirable. An assessment of this first phase can locate flaws that can be corrected before the program goes into full operation. The views of students, faculty, and program directors can be solicited regarding individual courses and the program as a whole. Observers can be enlisted to obtain the perspectives of those who have no direct investment in the program, even though they are members of the same institution. Analyses of student products, such as papers or exams, provide further information.

Once a program is initiated, a longitudinal study is desirable to follow student experiences over time: how, what, and when they study, their classroom participation, their relationships with faculty, and the growth of their competencies. (For an example of such research at Stanford, see note 24.) As students progress through college and into their postgraduate lives, the perceived value of their college experience and its general education component will evolve. By use of questionnaires and representative interviews at the end of each undergraduate year, near graduation, and some time after graduation, the changing perceptions and experiences of the students can be assessed. The involvement of graduates in the appraisal of their own education can bring about better ties between the institution and its alumni, fostering a feeling of intellectual kinship and of participation in shaping educational goals and values.

For faculty members, assessment is likely to provide its own education, and they should use it as a chance to generate incisive and insightful information on how the educational program can be made to work better. The assessment process also can furnish a theme for general education courses, such as an upper-division seminar on "Educational Self-assessment," which can bring together faculty from several disciplines. Such a seminar can include topics from data gathering and evaluation to probability arguments, estimation, historical and sociological principles, political sensitivity, and values. Students in the seminar can reflect on and assess their own college work and that of their peers while being exposed to problems similar in complexity to those they will confront as graduates. Such a seminar will impress on them the value of their general education and the necessity to retain the elasticity of their minds.

ASSURING ADMINISTRATIVE SUPPORT

Whenever a new idea or a new program is to be introduced into the curriculum or a new practice is proposed, we may expect some concern, anxiety, and resistance to follow. Where is the money going to come from? Who will do it? Is there space in an already crowded curriculum? Internal or external funding is frequently considered a precondition for the development and institutionalization of new ideas. Some faculty members may ask for released time, special compensation, and grant support. Others may want elaborate proofs of the viability of the program and strict evaluation procedures, even though they may not make the same demands concerning established programs.

Skillful administrators and faculty leaders anticipate and respond to these concerns. To overcome faculty hesitation about initiating experimental efforts because of fear they may jeopardize their chances for reappointment or promotion, effective administrators make it clear that these efforts will be rewarded rather than penalized. They provide structures and moral and financial support that may be modest but crucial. By devoting even a small percentage of the annual academic budget to educational innovation, they can achieve impressive results. They also recognize

The task of reconsidering and reshaping the means we employ in educating our students has only begun

the individuality and even idiosyncrasy of experimentally oriented faculty and devise pluralistic approaches to experimentation rather than seeking one formula to which all subscribe. They may even teach or take a course each year as a way to stay intellectually fresh and up to date.

Curricular change and revitalization are best assured when administrators and faculty collaborate. The major new general education program of Miami-Dade Community College can be attributed in large part to such collaboration. Roles of administrators and faculty in the planning process can vary depending on the traditions and ethos of the institution. On some campuses, administrators need to play a less visible role than on others, relying on faculty members whose effectiveness depends upon persuasion, friendship, and alliances. On all campuses, faculty need to be groomed for this task.

Many observers have called attention to the crucial role of administrative leadership in bringing about educational change. The question of leadership in any democratic organization or society is a vexing one. This is especially true with respect to colleges and universities, which tend toward anarchism. Faced by anarchy, academic administrators may be tempted to be autocratic, but that temptation must be resisted. They may forget that their function is not just to manage but to inspire. What is called for are leaders who have what James MacGregor Burns calls the capacity for "transforming leadership"—people who gain allegiance by their ability to articulate goals that express the intent and fulfill the potential of the governed.[25] Such leadership requires observation, consultation, and, above all, the continual empowerment of the governed.

REVITALIZING GENERAL EDUCATION

In 1962, the scholar Robert H. Knapp characterized American higher education as having gone through three historic phases. The first, which lasted well into the nineteenth century, he labelled the "pastoral" or character-developing phase. The second emphasized the transmission of knowledge, while the third and current period is dominated by research and the generation of new knowledge.[26] Even today, however, the pastoral American ideal of college as shaping character and developing responsible citizenship remains alive. The 1960s brought renewed emphasis on the personal and social responsibilities of the college and its students. The 1970s and early 1980s witnessed some retreat from this emphasis as students turned more and more attention to career preparation, but as the resurgence of faculty interest in general education showed, faculty retained a concern for student development beyond job skills and specialized knowledge.

In 1986, Benno Schmidt, the new president of Yale, one of the nation's preeminent centers of research, emphasized in his inaugural address the development of moral purpose as the fundamental goal of undergraduate education. He went so far as to suggest that the very neutrality of intellect, its remoteness from the issues and concerns of everyday life, may have been a factor in undercutting the moral mission of higher education, given bitter evidence in the prostration of universities and scholars to totalitarian regimes.[27] While President Schmidt would undoubtedly be among the first to assert that such neutrality and detachment gives scholarship its special power to achieve objectivity and analytic depth, he called attention to a purpose that may be crowded out by the busyness of scholarship and the massive glut of information and techniques.

Schmidt is not alone. Even though students remain concerned about job placement, the available evidence shows that they want college not only to prepare them for careers but also to help them become intellec-

tually more sophisticated, to grow in their capacity for relationships, to encounter people different from themselves, and to develop emotionally. Though far fewer freshmen today than fifteen years ago view college as an opportunity to develop a meaningful philosophy of life, at least 40 percent of them still hold this view.[28]

Thus we see prospects of new excitement and vitality in undergraduate education and liberal learning. We sense lively debate and invigorated practice at those institutions in which faculty are willing to engage in the necessarily prolonged analyses of and experimentation in general education courses and programs. We hope that the national discussion about undergraduate education of which this publication is a part will help renew the ideal of a community of scholars, and will strengthen cooperation across disciplines and departments in contrast to the isolation that has recently characterized so much of academic life. The task of reconsidering and reshaping the means we employ in educating our students has only begun. Much work remains for all of us, and it holds the promise that we will not only become more effective as teachers but experience more pleasure and excitement in our lives as faculty.

REFERENCES

1. Study of Educational Policy and Outcomes, *Recommendations on the Core Curriculum* (Philadelphia: St. Joseph's University, October 1987).

2. Elizabeth Coleman, "The Rhetoric and Realities of Reform in Higher Education" (Keynote address, Wingspread Conference on the Undergraduate Curriculum, Racine, Wisc., 1982), 16.

3. John M. Braxton and Robert C. Nordvall, "Selective Liberal Arts Colleges: Higher Quality as Well as Higher Prestige?" *Journal of Higher Education* 56 (September/October 1985): 538–554.

4. *Introduction to the Core Curriculum: A Guide for Freshmen*, (Cambridge, Mass.: Harvard University Press), 4.

5. H. E. Gruber and J. J. Vonèche, eds., *The Essential Piaget* (New York: Basic Books, 1977); and William Perry, *Forms of Intellectual and Ethical Development in the College Years* (New York: Holt, Rinehart & Winston, Inc., 1970).

6. Margaret L. Andersen, "Changing the Curriculum in Higher Education," *Signs: Journal of Women in Culture and Society* 12 (Winter 1982): 222–254.

7. Ann Fausto-Sterling, personal communication and *Myths of Gender* (New York: Basic Books, 1985).

8. *Integrity in the College Curriculum* (Washington, D.C.: Association of American Colleges, 1985), 15–23. The other reports in chronological order are:
□ Study Group on the Condition of Excellence in American Higher Education, *Involvement in Learning* (Washington, D.C.: National Institute of Education, 1984).
□ William J. Bennett, *To Reclaim a Legacy* (Washington, D.C.: National Endowment for the Humanities, 1984).
□ Frank Newman, *Higher Education and the American Resurgence* (Princeton: The Carnegie Foundation for the Advancement of Teaching, 1985).
□ Ernest L. Boyer, *College: The Undergraduate Experience in America* (New York: Harper & Row, 1987).
□ Arthur W. Chickering and Zelda F. Gamson, "Seven Principles for Good Practice in Undergraduate Education," *AAHE Bulletin* 39 (March 1987): 3–7.

9. Patrick Hill, "Inter-Generational Communities: Partnerships in Discovery," in *Against the Current: Reforms and Experimentation in Higher Education*, eds. R. Jones and B. Smith (Cambridge: Schenkman Books, Inc., 1984).

10. Recent research on comprehension and memory is reviewed in Richard E. Mayer, *Thinking, Problem Solving, Cognition* (New York: W. H. Freeman and Co., 1983), see especially 229–233.

11. Roland Christensen, "Foreword," in *The Art and Craft of Teaching*, ed. Margaret M. Gullette (Cambridge: Harvard-Danforth Center for Teaching and Learning, 1982), xiv.

12. Donald L. Finkel and G.

REFERENCES

Stephen Monk, "Teaching and Learning Groups: Dissolution of the Atlas Complex," in *Learning in Groups: New Directions for Teaching and Learning 14*, eds. Clark Bouton and Russell Y. Garth (San Francisco: Jossey-Bass, 1983), 83–97.

13. Ernest A. Lynton, "Strengthening the Connection Between Campus and Business," *Forum for Liberal Education* 8 (January/February 1986): 2–4.

14. Karen T. Romer, *Models of Collaboration in Undergraduate Education* (Providence: Brown University, 1985).

15. Joseph Katz, "Learning to Help Students Learn," *Liberal Education* 73 (January/February 1987): 28–30.

16. R. E. Snow and D. F. Lohman, "Toward a Theory of Cognitive Aptitude for Learning from Instruction," *Journal of Educational Psychology* 76 (June 1984): 347–376.

17. Charles S. Claxton and Patricia H. Murrell, *Learning Styles: Implications for Educational Practices*, no. 4 in the *1987 ASHE-ERIC Higher Education Reports* series (Washington, D.C.: Association for the Study of Higher Education, 1988).

18. Alexander W. Astin, *Four Critical Years: Effects of College on Beliefs, Attitudes, and Knowledge* (San Francisco: Jossey-Bass, 1977); Mary F. Belenky et al., *Women's Ways of Knowing* (New York: Basic Books, 1986); Arthur W. Chickering, ed., *The Modern American College* (San Francisco: Jossey-Bass, 1981); Mervin B. Freedman, *The College Experience* (San Francisco: Jossey-Bass, 1967); Nevitt Sanford, ed., *The American College: A Psychological and Social Interpretation of the Higher Learning* (New York: John Wiley & Sons, Inc., 1962); and Mina P. Shaughnessy, *Errors and Expectations* (New York: Oxford University Press, 1977).

19. Howard Gardner, *Frames of Mind* (New York: Basic Books, 1983).

20. Project Panel on the General Professional Education of the Physician and College Preparation for Medicine, "Physicians for the Twenty-First Century," Part Two, *Journal of Medical Education* 59 (November 1984): 11.

21. Kenneth A. Feldman and Theodore M. Newcomb, *The Impact of College on Students* (San Francisco: Jossey-Bass, 1969).

22. Nevitt Sanford, ed., *The American College* (New York: John Wiley & Sons, Inc., 1962), 432.

23. The work of C. Robert Pace provides valuable guidelines. See his chapter on "Perspectives and Problems in Student Outcomes Research," in *Assessing Educational Outcomes: New Directions for Institutional Research* 47, ed. P. T. Ewell (San Francisco: Jossey-Bass, 1985), 7–18.

24. Herent A. Katchadourian et al., *Careerism and Intellectualism Among College Students: Patterns of Academic and Career Choice in the Undergraduate Years* (San Francisco: Jossey-Bass,

1985).

25. James MacGregor Burns, *Leadership* (New York: Harper & Row, 1978).

26. Robert H. Knapp, "Changing Functions of the College Professor," in *The American College*, ed. Nevitt Sanford (New York: John Wiley & Sons, Inc., 1962), 290–311.

27. Benno Schmidt, quoted in *New York Times*, 21 September 1986, sec. 1, p. 40.

28. Alexander W. Astin et al., *The American Freshman: National Norms* (Los Angeles: Higher Education Research Institute, 1986).